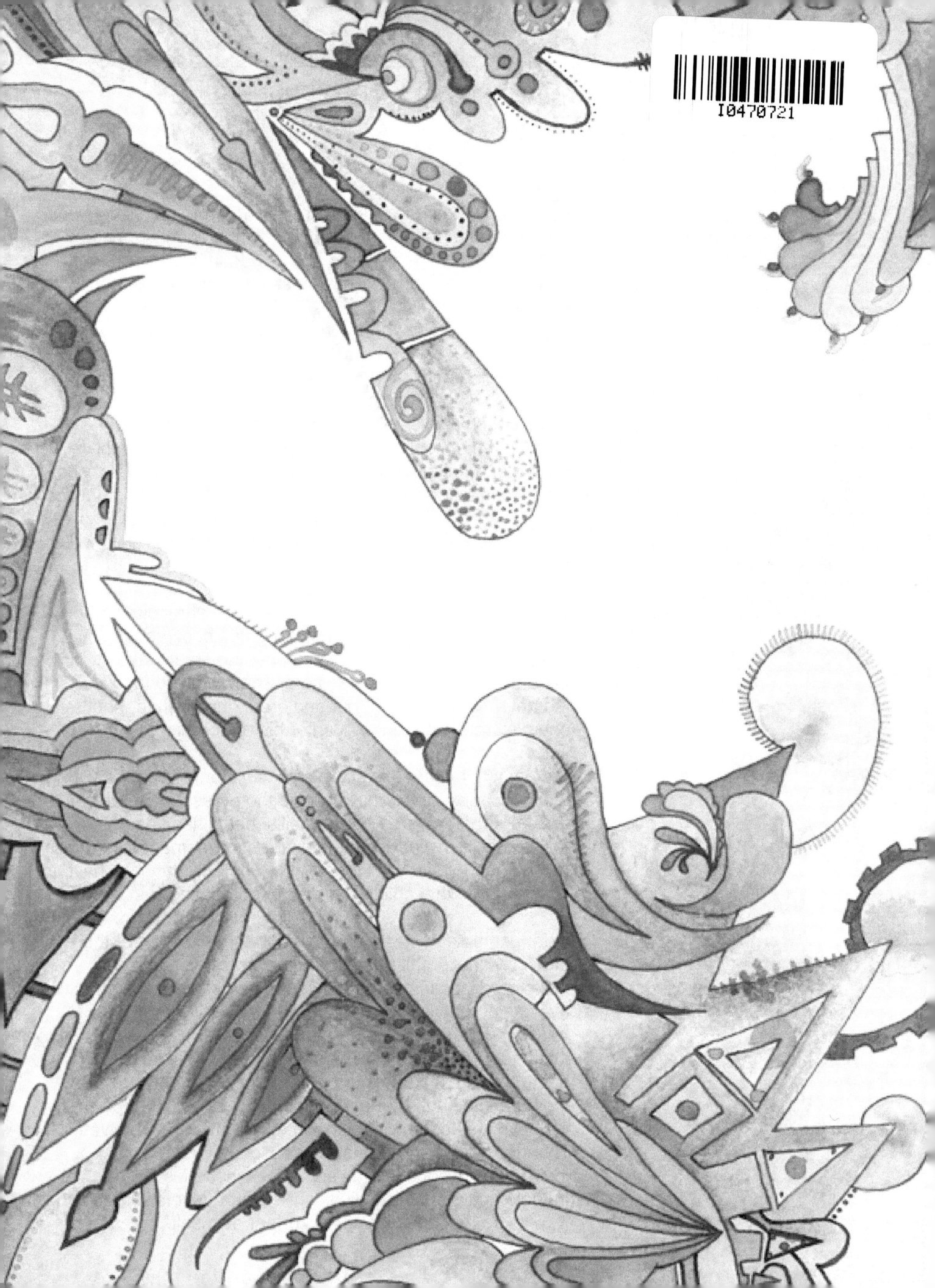

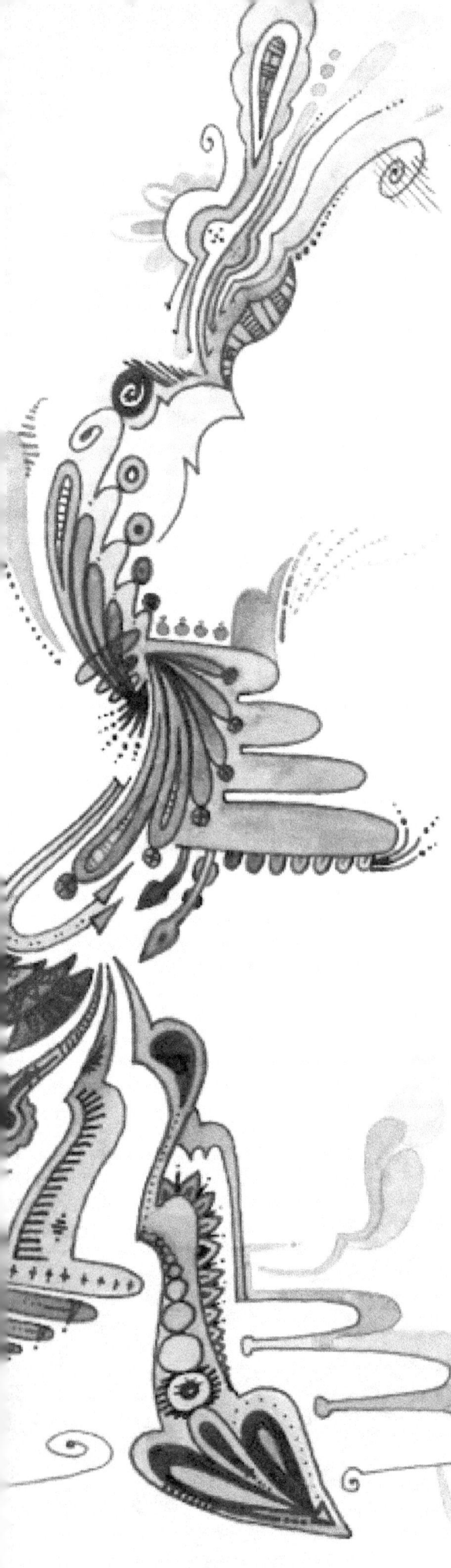

Color Your Way to Creative Consciousness!

(A note from Sudevi)

Welcome to an adventure in line and color!

Many of my YouTube viewers have written to me asking what they can do to regain the playfulness and spontaneity they had as little children. Others ask how to invigorate the right-brain (creative mind) when almost everything in their daily routine is formulaic. Still more want to know how to relax and enjoy their evenings after stressful days at work or school.

This coloring book is my answer to all of those questions!

If you watch a little child, especially one who hasn't yet entered the school system, or who happens to be in the middle of a holiday break, you can easily see that he or she lives life in a carefree and relaxed way. While playing outside, talking with other little ones, helping a parent with chores, or sitting at the table engaged in arts and crafts, the child will be in the present moment.

When a child sits down with a blank page or a coloring book, he or she will not be filled with thoughts about what else needs to be done, or with stress over the time it takes to finish the project at hand. Instead, he or she will be so focused (sometimes with tongue out and drool dripping!) that not even one disturbing thought can enter his or her mind.

We often think that this state is possible only for those young ones because they don't yet have the pressures of the world to deal with; they are free from bills, deadlines and responsibilities- but actually, this present-moment awareness can be had by all. And I mean ALL. The only thing we have to do to get into that childlike zone, is "something."

If, for example, instead of flipping on the television at the end of a long day, or falling onto the couch with a magazine or newspaper, we instead choose to occupy our minds creatively by writing, drawing, painting, or- yes- creatively coloring, we will soon find that the lethargy and inner torment so often taken for granted as 'normal' in adulthood will diminish. Part of the reason so many people think there's nothing to do if they aren't being entertained from an outside source is that we have lost touch with our own ability to keep ourselves engaged. We think of ourselves as 'consumers,' not 'producers.' A consumer is someone who relies on the outpourings of others to live, while a producer is someone who takes responsibility for his or her own self.

If you go through a newspaper or a magazine, flipping from page to page until you grow bored with it, and then you throw it in the trash, you have 'consumed' it. However, if you take a sheet of paper, and on that page, you write a story or a poem, or you draw a picture or a doodle, then you save that page as an expression of your creative self, you have 'produced' a work. When we are productive, we feel good about ourselves, and when we feel good about ourselves, we are less likely to fall into stress and malaise.

For some, though, facing a blank page with the intention of 'making' something out of it feels as daunting as looking up at Mount Everest without the proper hiking equipment.

This is where creative coloring comes in.

Creative coloring is coloring without the 'rules' of coloring.

In most coloring books, definitive lines exist and shapes must be filled with flat colors. In this book, though, ample opportunity is left within each hand drawn page for your own expression to come through. On the cover image, for example, you can see that colored shapes have been created within the line drawn shapes, and small details have been added. This same way, you are invited to make these pictures your own! You can color in the ordinary way if you wish to, or, you can draw around the drawings, mix multiple colors within the same forms, fill in the negative space while leaving the positive space as it is or vice versa, overdraw the outlines with thick markers to make them more prominent, and so on. Once you get going, there's no limit to your creativity.

May you discover a love for this unique form of creative expression, and find that each piece is a gateway to the meditative, present-moment consciousness of a playful child! And don't let my lines limit you- I would consider this book a great success if those of you who have it are inspired to do drawings and coloring sheets of your own, too.

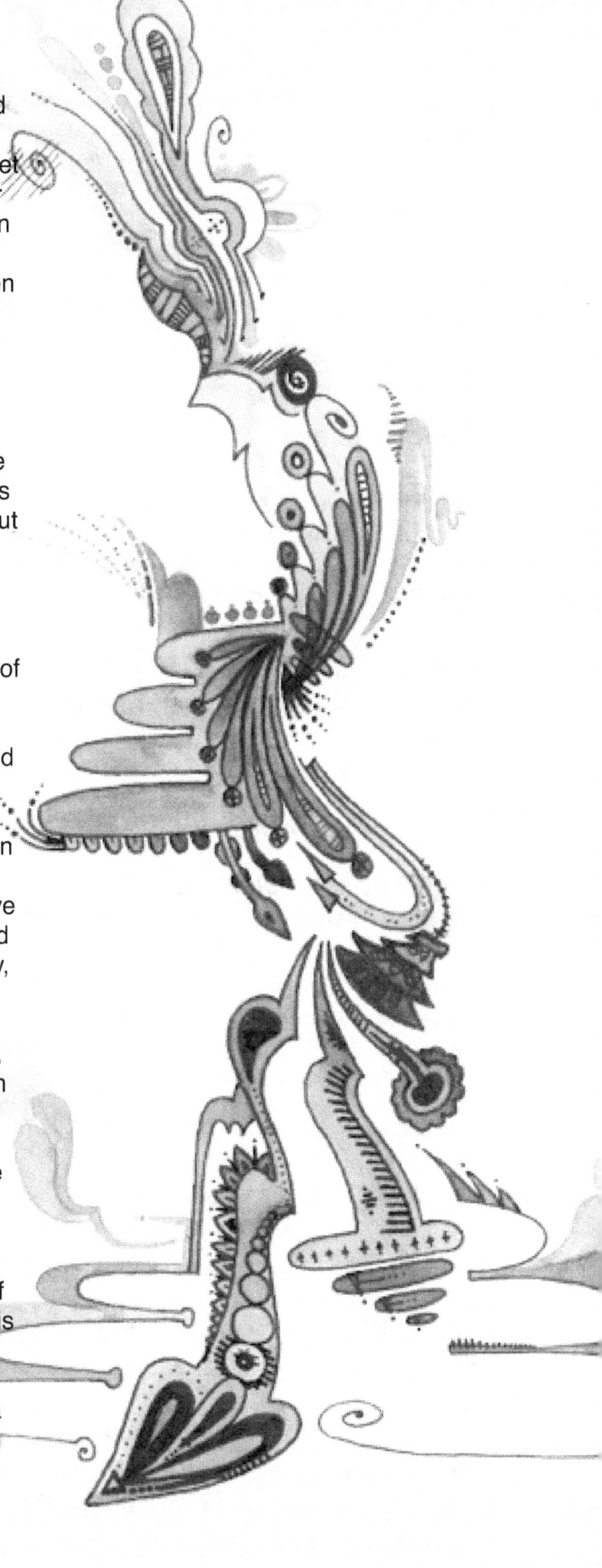

Fun Facts about Coloring and the Brain

Kyung Hee Kim, an educational psychologist, participated in a question and answer session for *Britannica* which addressed the widespread decline of children's creativity in America. Kim attributes the downfall of creative expression to the large number of children who have abandoned creative hobbies and replaced them with hours of mind-numbing television and video games. She argues that although video games may take place in fantasy environments, they do not foster actual creativity because there are a set number of solutions within each game, and children are playing them at a prime time for creative development. Since creativity is directly related to our problem solving skills, it stands to reason that our time will be much better used by making something without creative boundaries, than by merely watching something someone else has made.

"Imagination is more important than knowledge." Albert Einstein

Doodling allows the right brain to play while also occupying the left brain. Experts say that by regularly doodling, which means, drawing freely without paying attention to the end result of the image, or pre-planning the composition, helps train the brain in creative problem solving. "You may find that the solution to problems come to you when you take breaks to doodle," says brain researcher Regina Paul. Actually, all the coloring pages in this book are 'doodles,' and the book itself can be called a 'Doodling Book' as easily as it's called a 'Coloring Book.' If you'd like to doodle, simply draw freely around the shapes already on the pages, and enjoy! Some pages were created especially for doodling and drawing; specifically, the circles on pages 20, 21 and 22 can be filled in with your own art, as can be the frame on page 23, and all of the many 'partial page' drawings, which leave ample room for you to stretch your creative powers. You'll also find the very last page is empty, ready for you to make with it whatever you will!

"If you hear a voice within you say, 'You cannot paint,' then by all means paint, and that voice will be silenced." – Vincent Van Gogh"

Development of ideas and the actualization of thoughts into form is done by the the right brain while the left brain is responsible for technicalities like hand eye co-ordination and following set rules. For this reason, coloring can't be called a 'right brain' activity alone; it's a whole brain activity. While your right brain is being creative, deciding which colors to put where, how to blend and pattern them, and whether to use harmonious colors or shockingly opposite ones, the left brain is active in guiding your hand to put the pencil, brush or marker where you want it, and to keep the final piece within the realm of the visualization made by the right brain. Those who have both left and right brain working in sync find answers to problems most quickly, and also find the ability to take action when action needs to be taken without stress or procrastination.

"Every child is an artist, the problem is staying an artist when you grow up." – Pablo Picasso

In the Bible, Jesus famously said, "Truly I tell you, unless you change and become like little children, you will never enter the kingdom of heaven." What better way to become like a little child, then by doing what little children do- be creative, and enjoy!

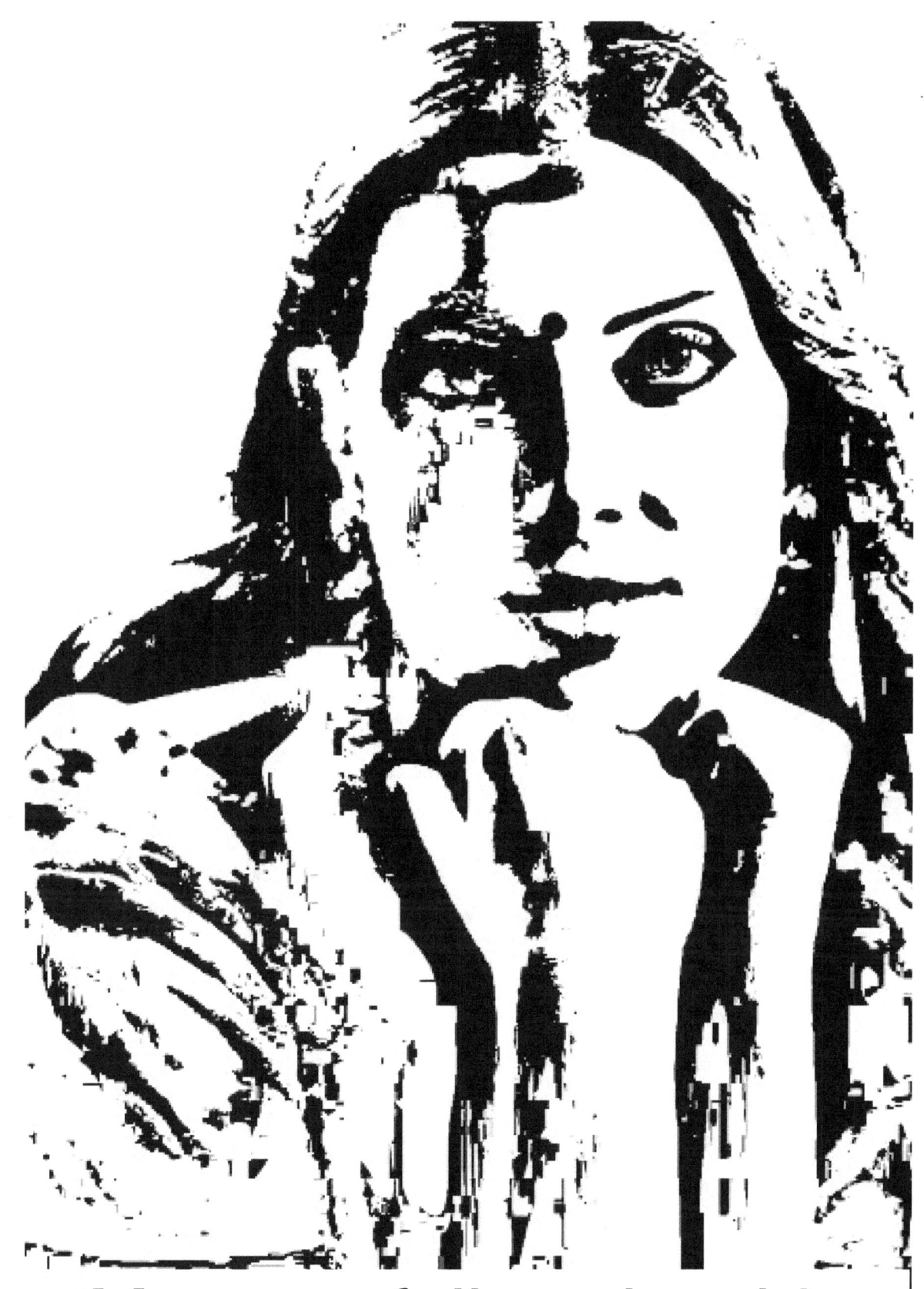

May you fully enjoy this colouring experience!

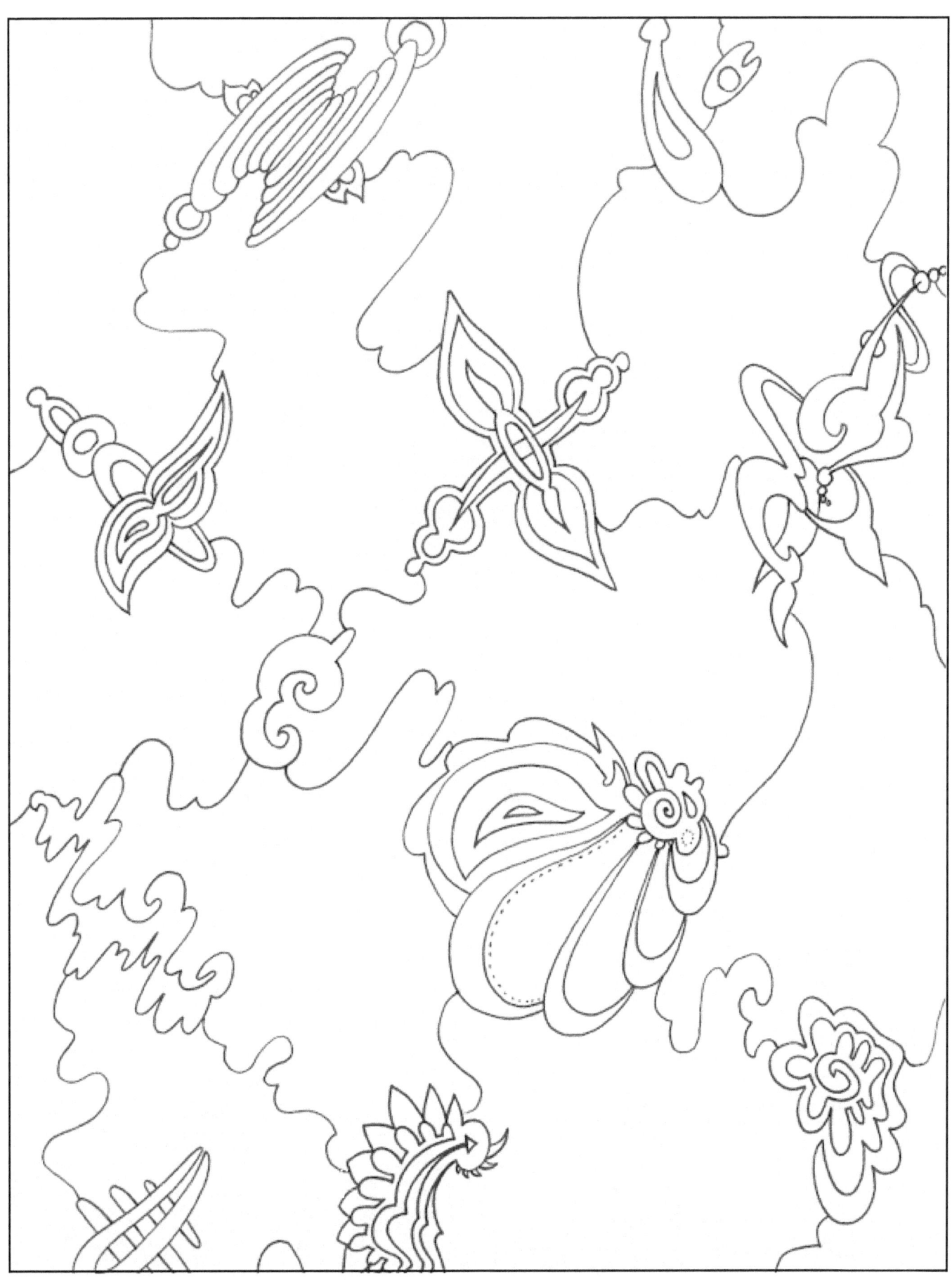

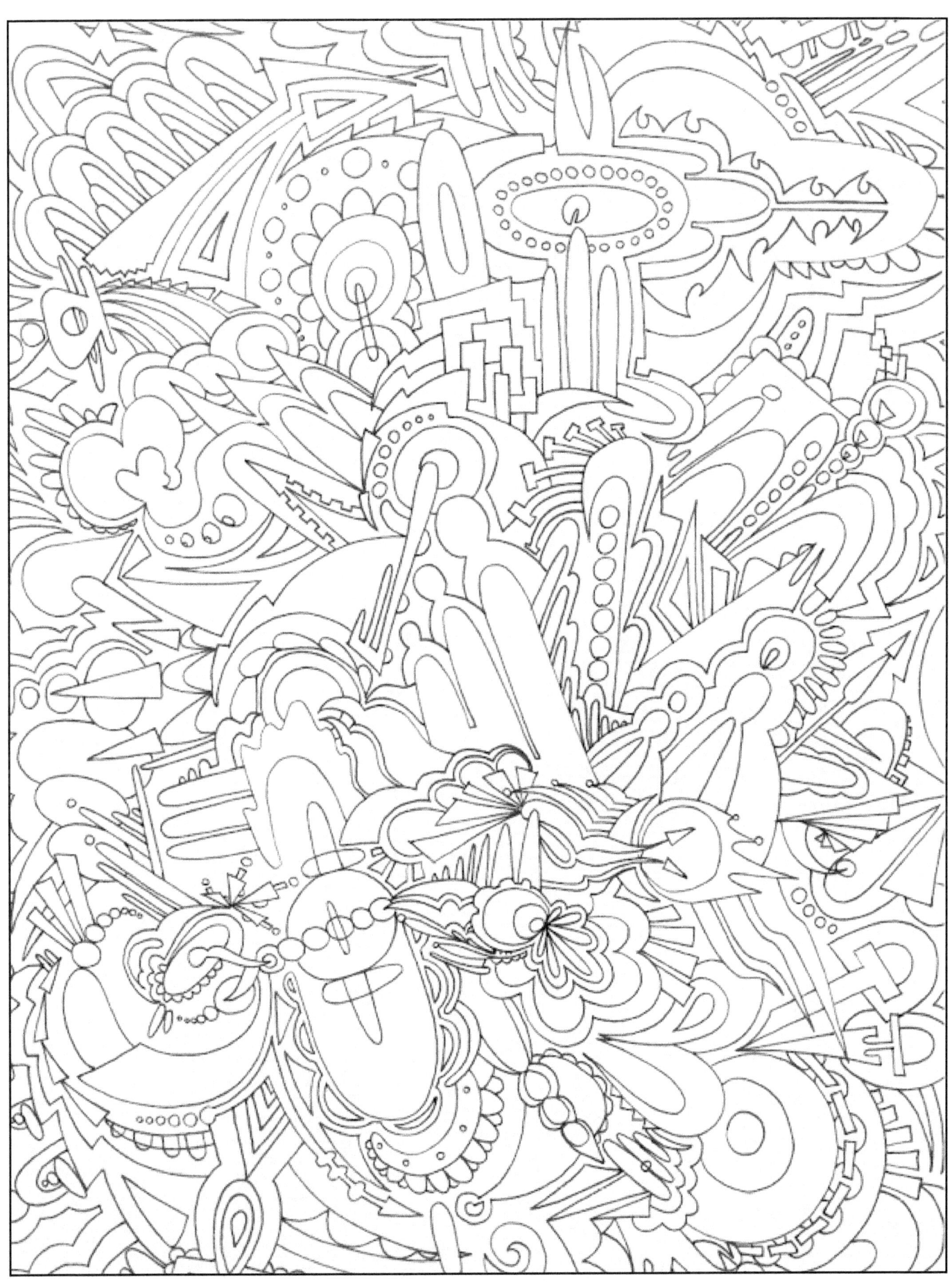

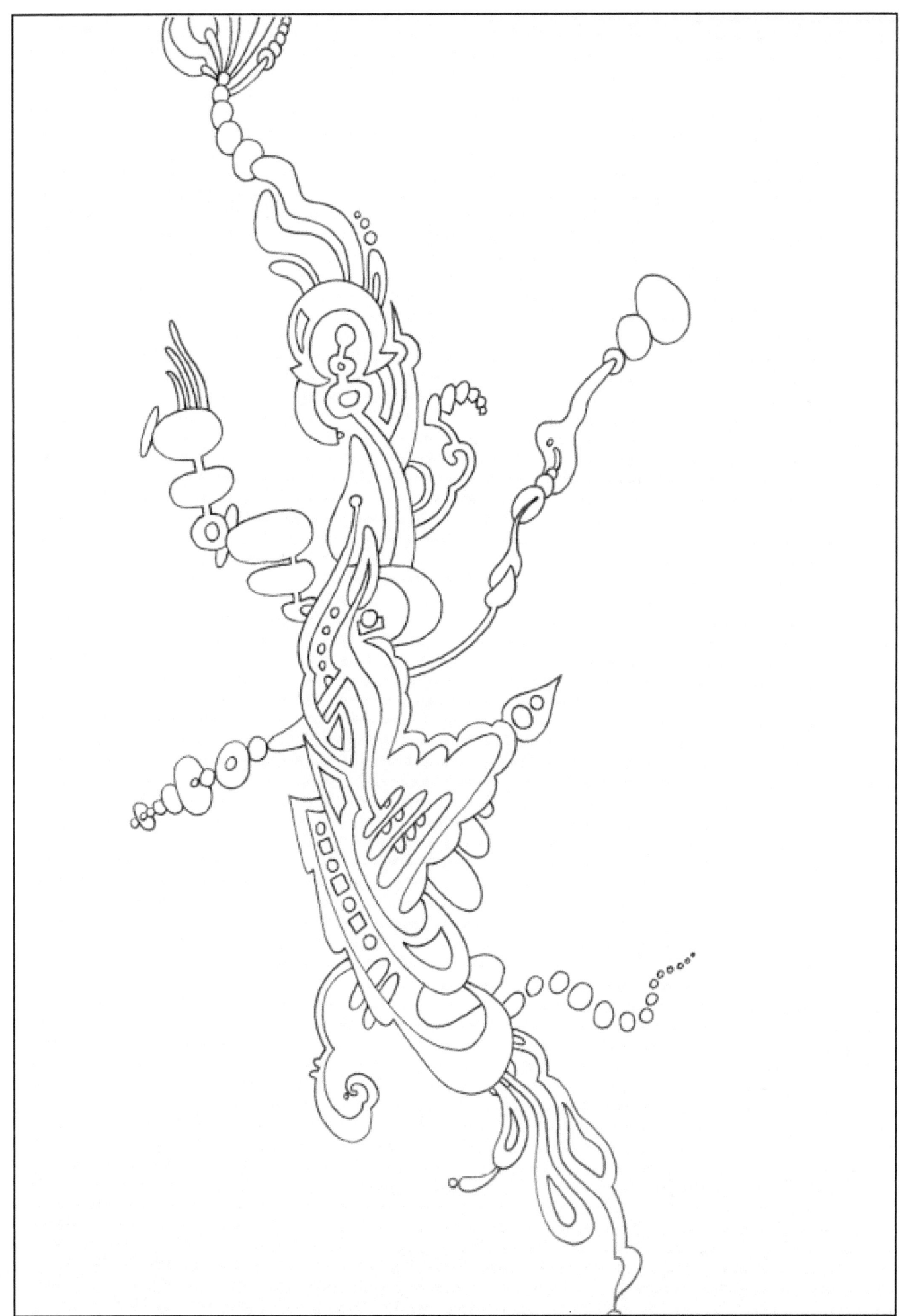

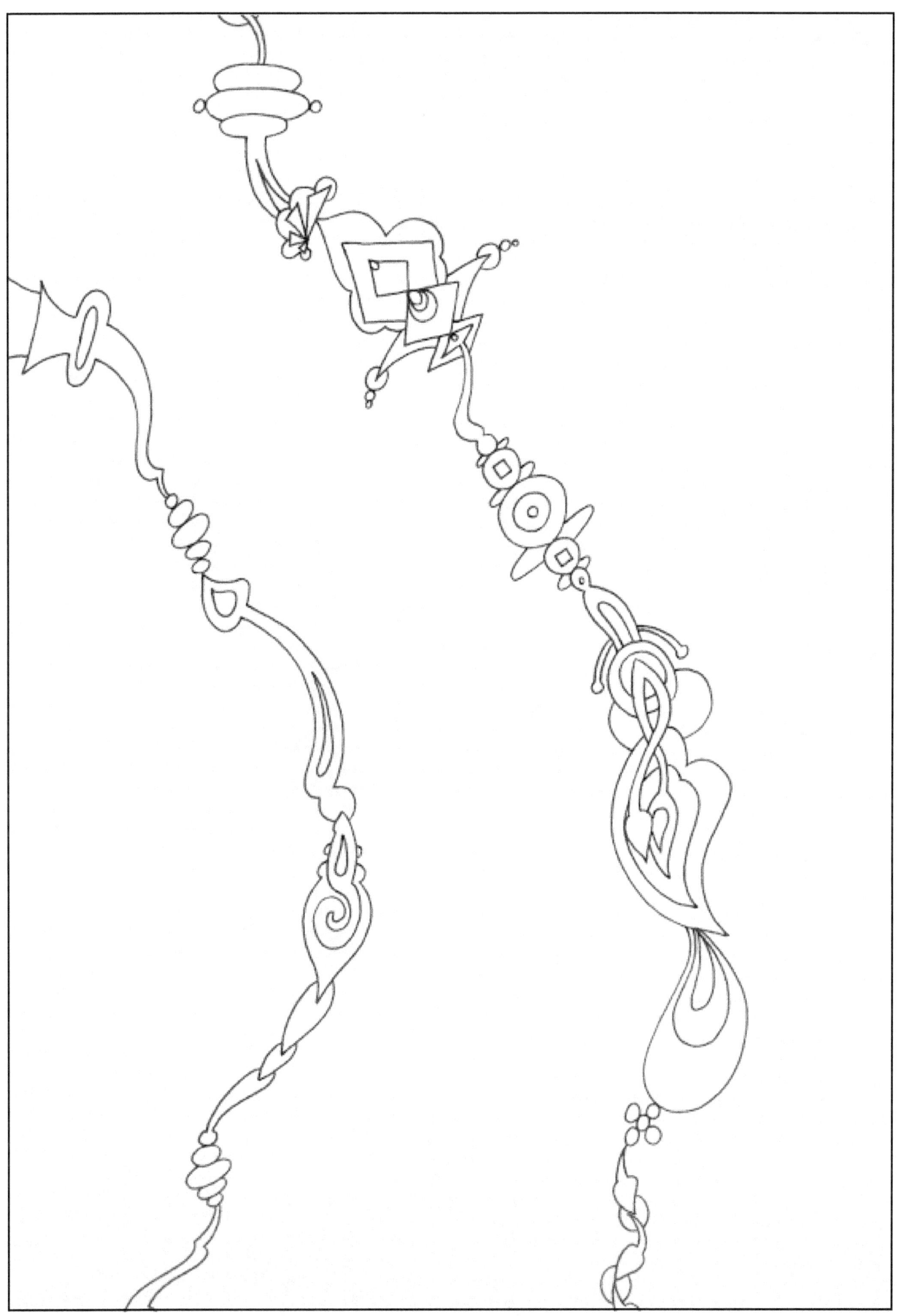

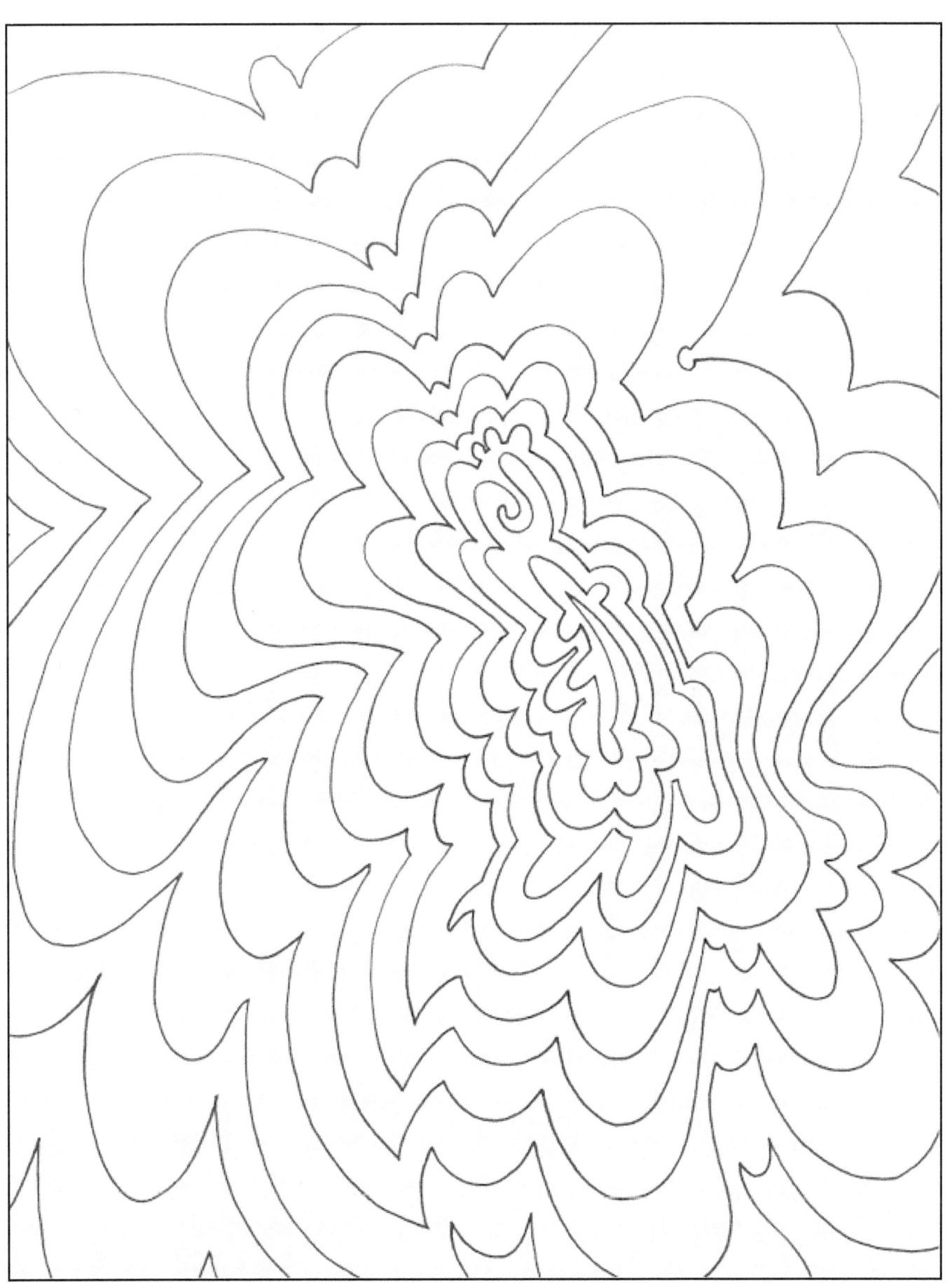

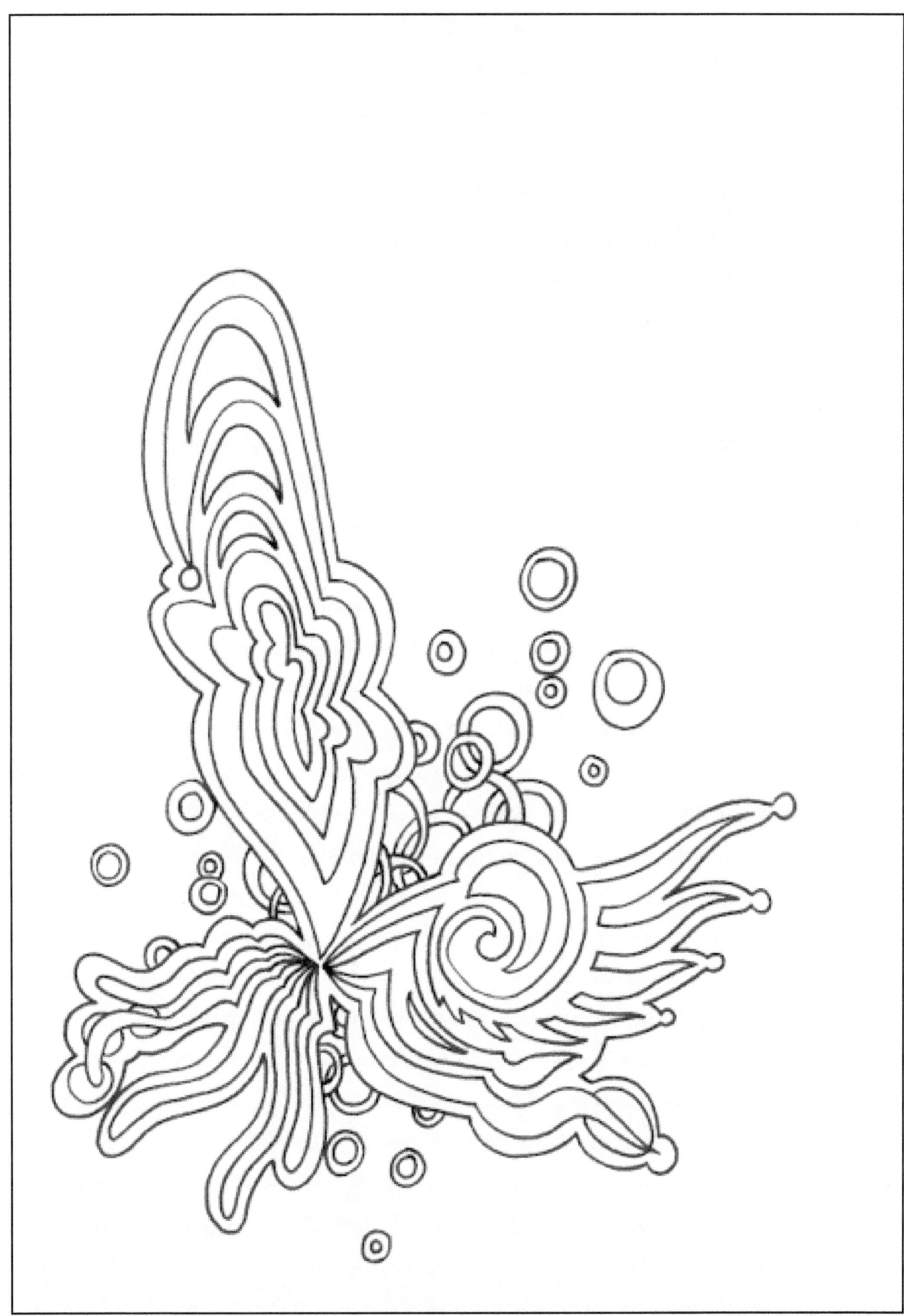

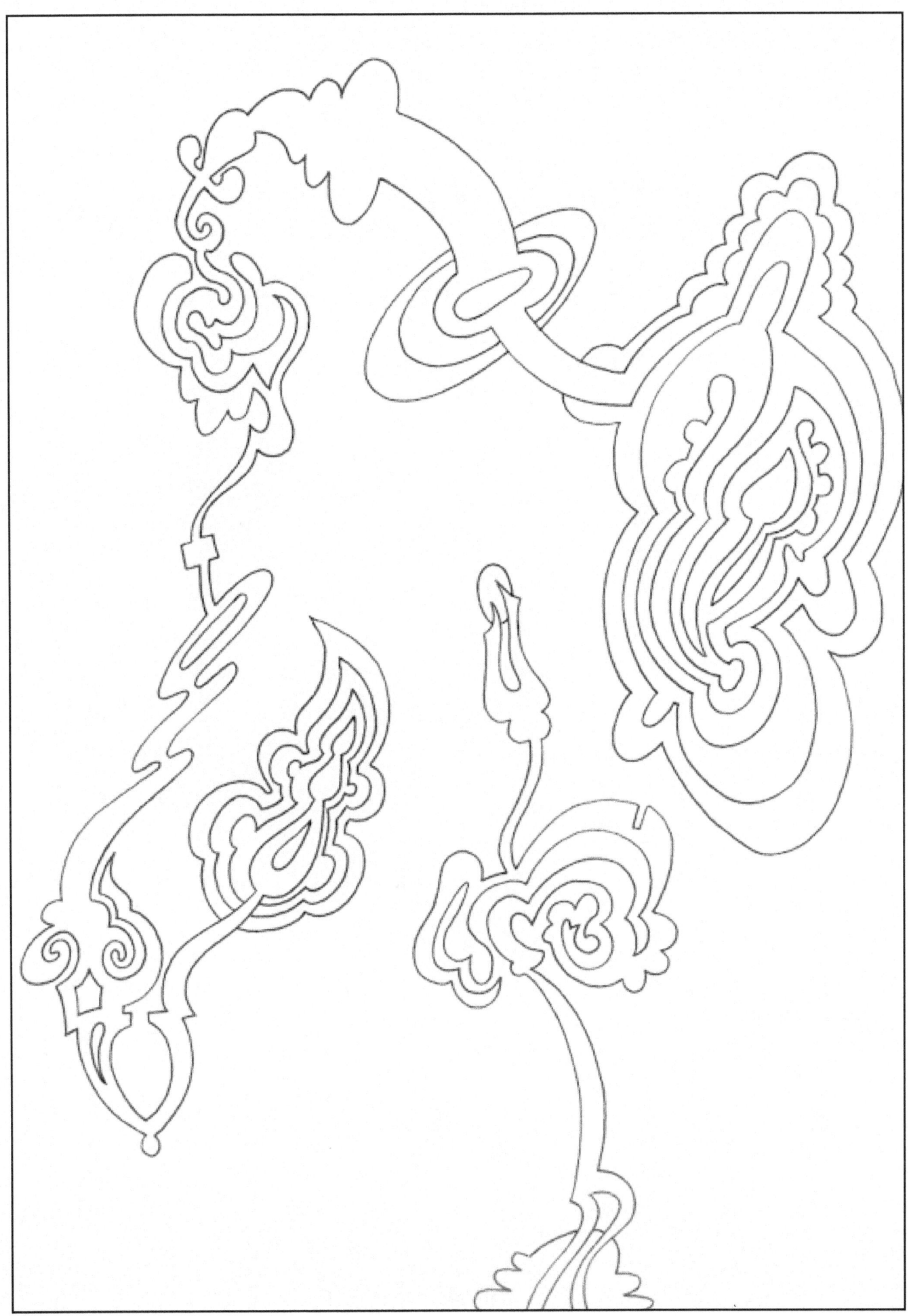

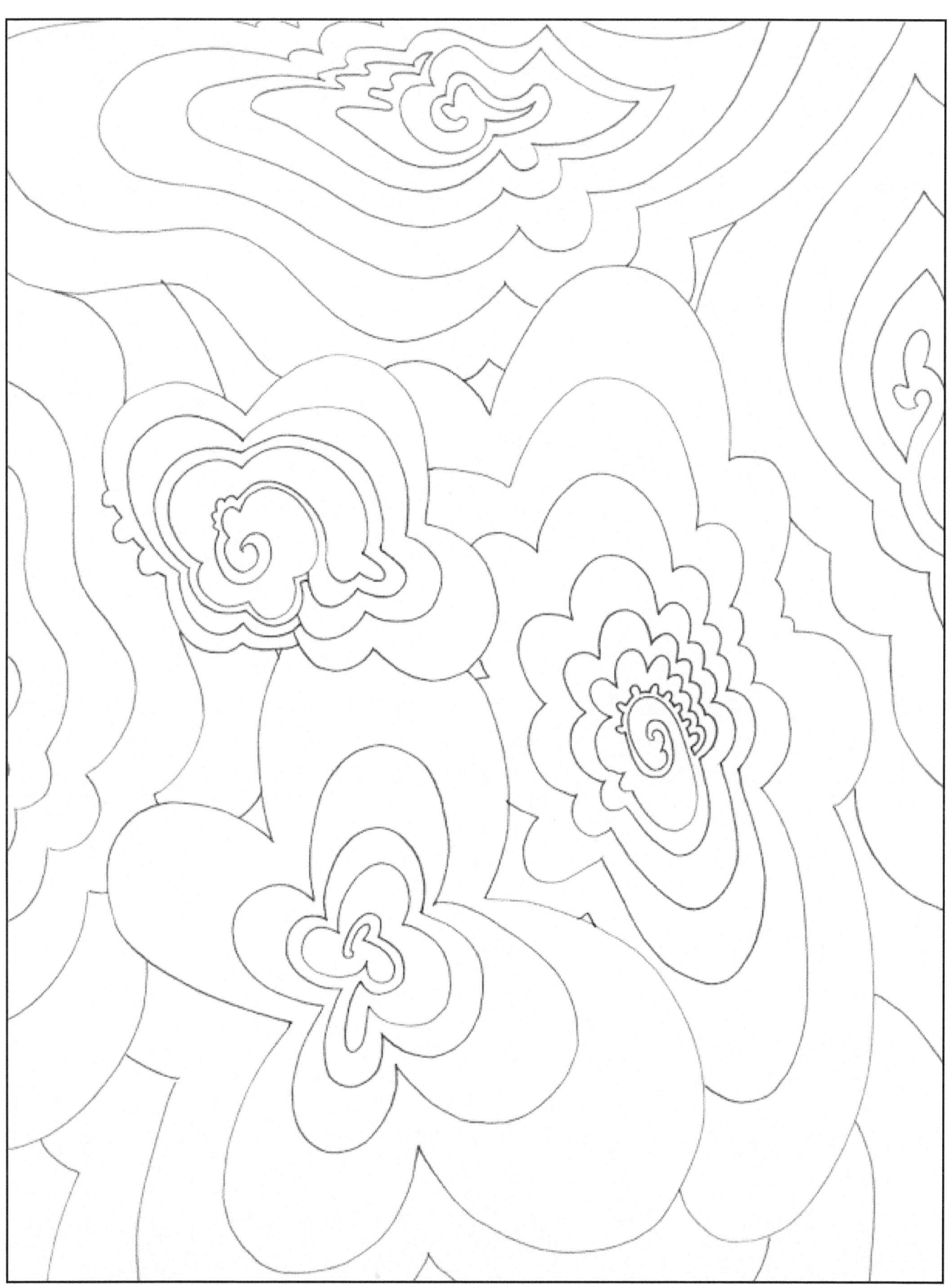

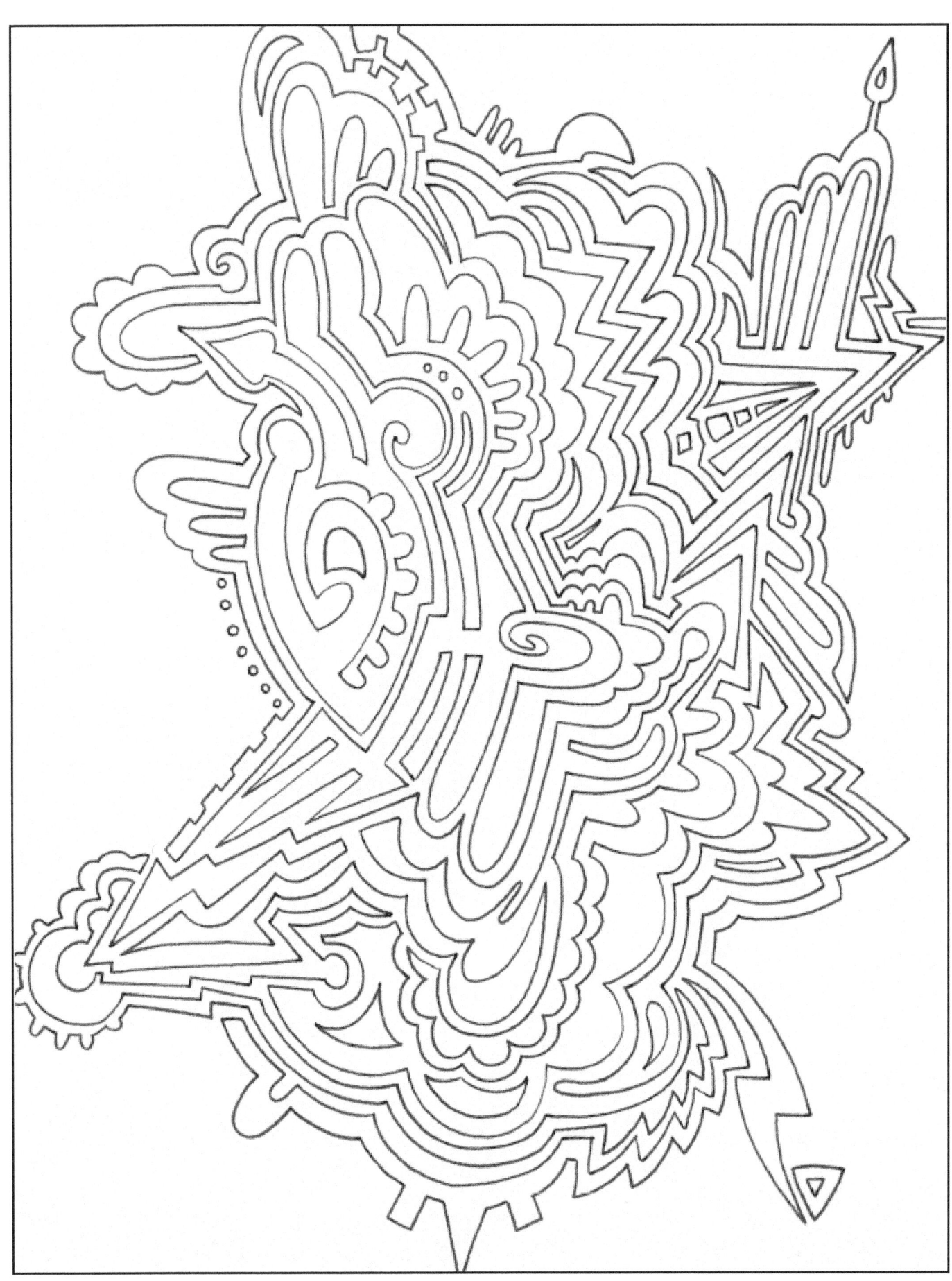

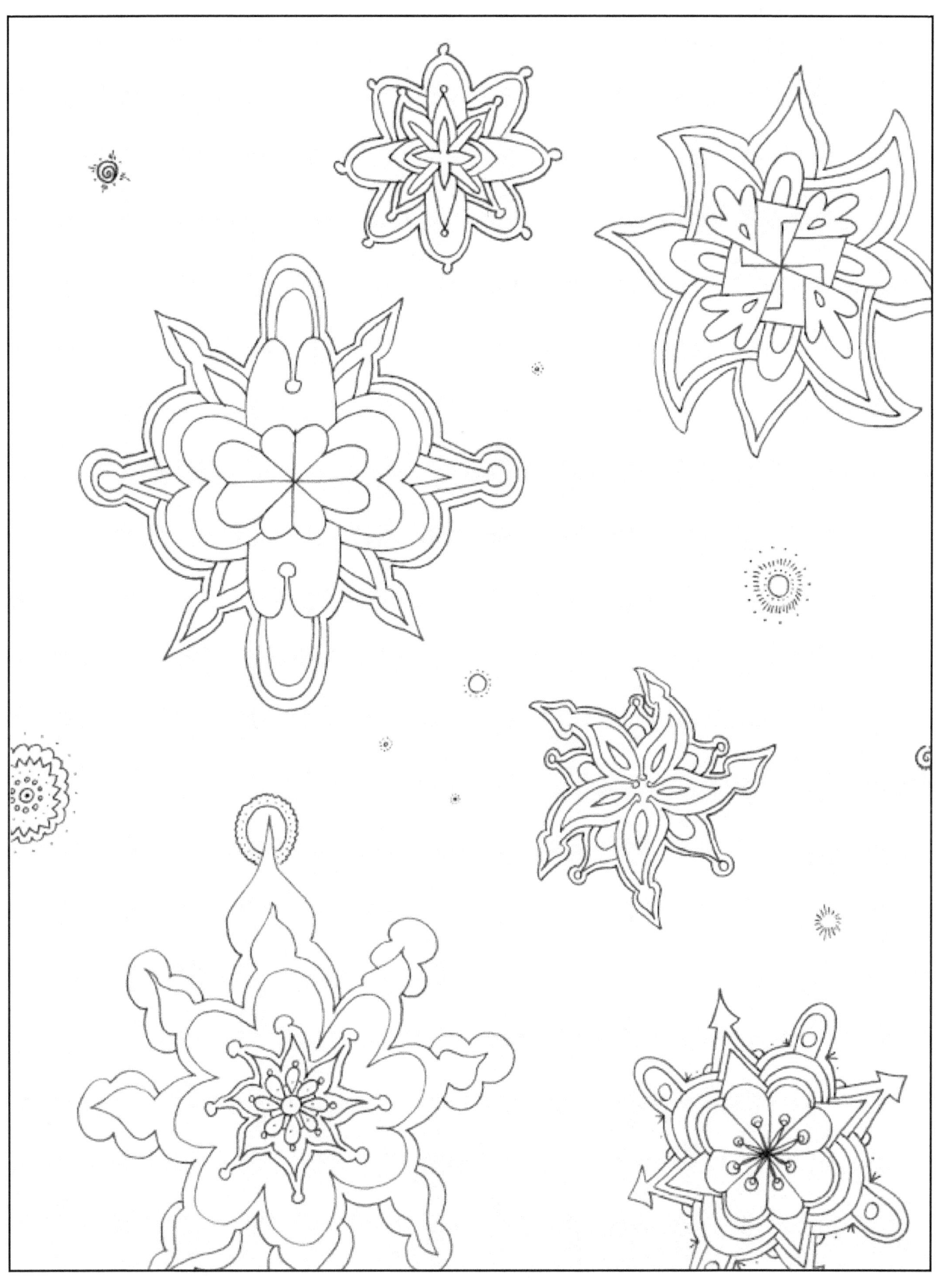

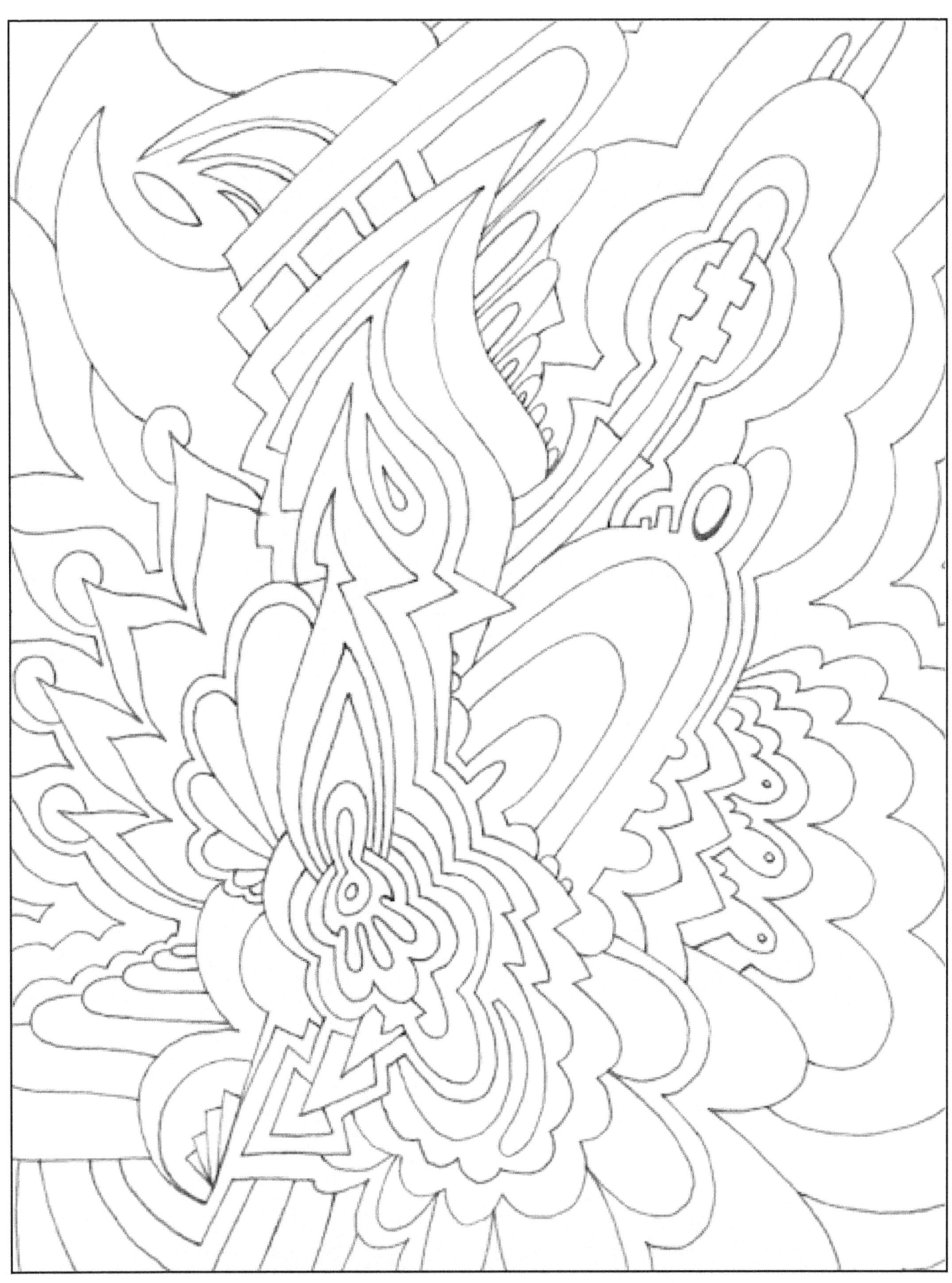

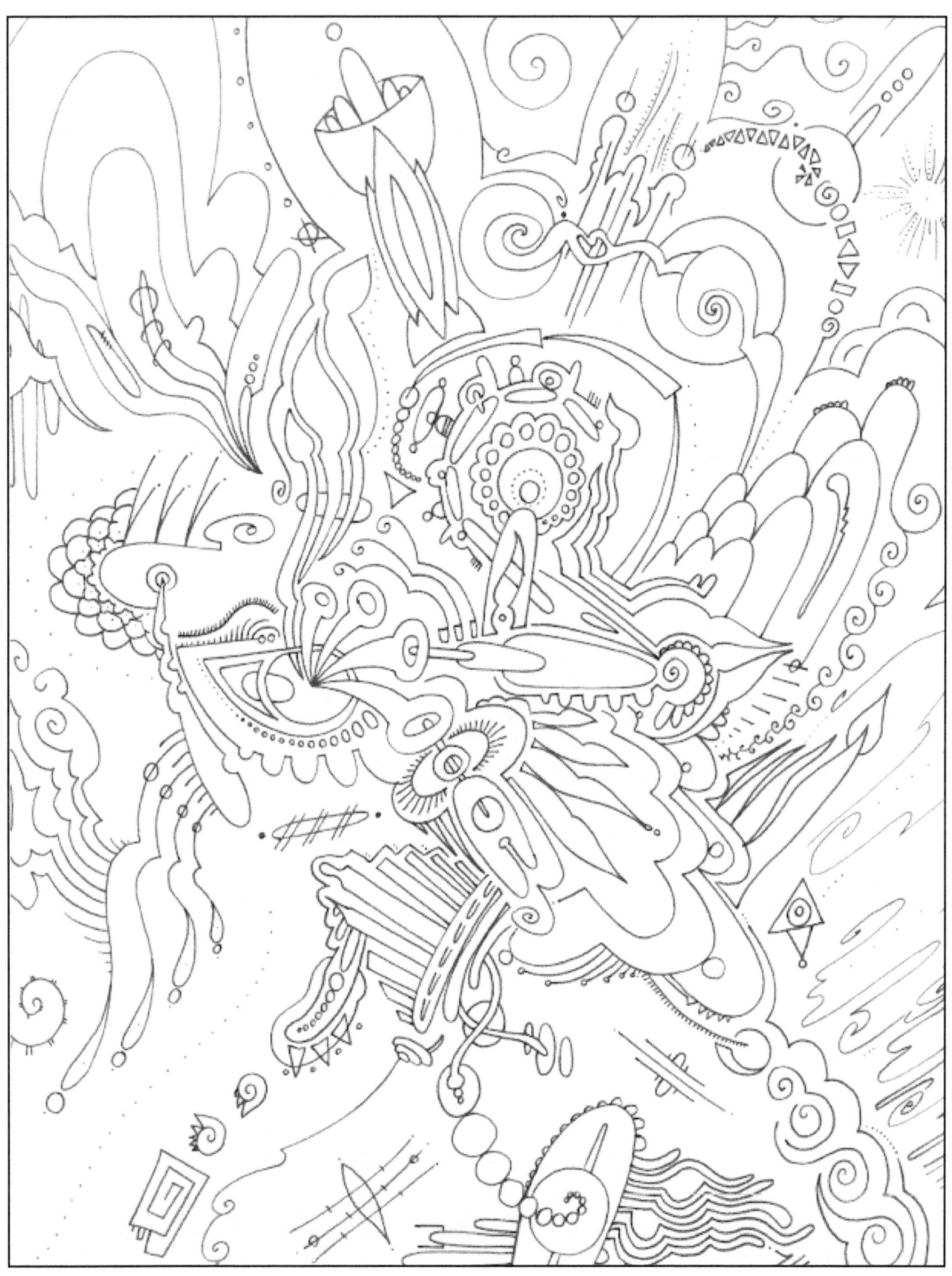

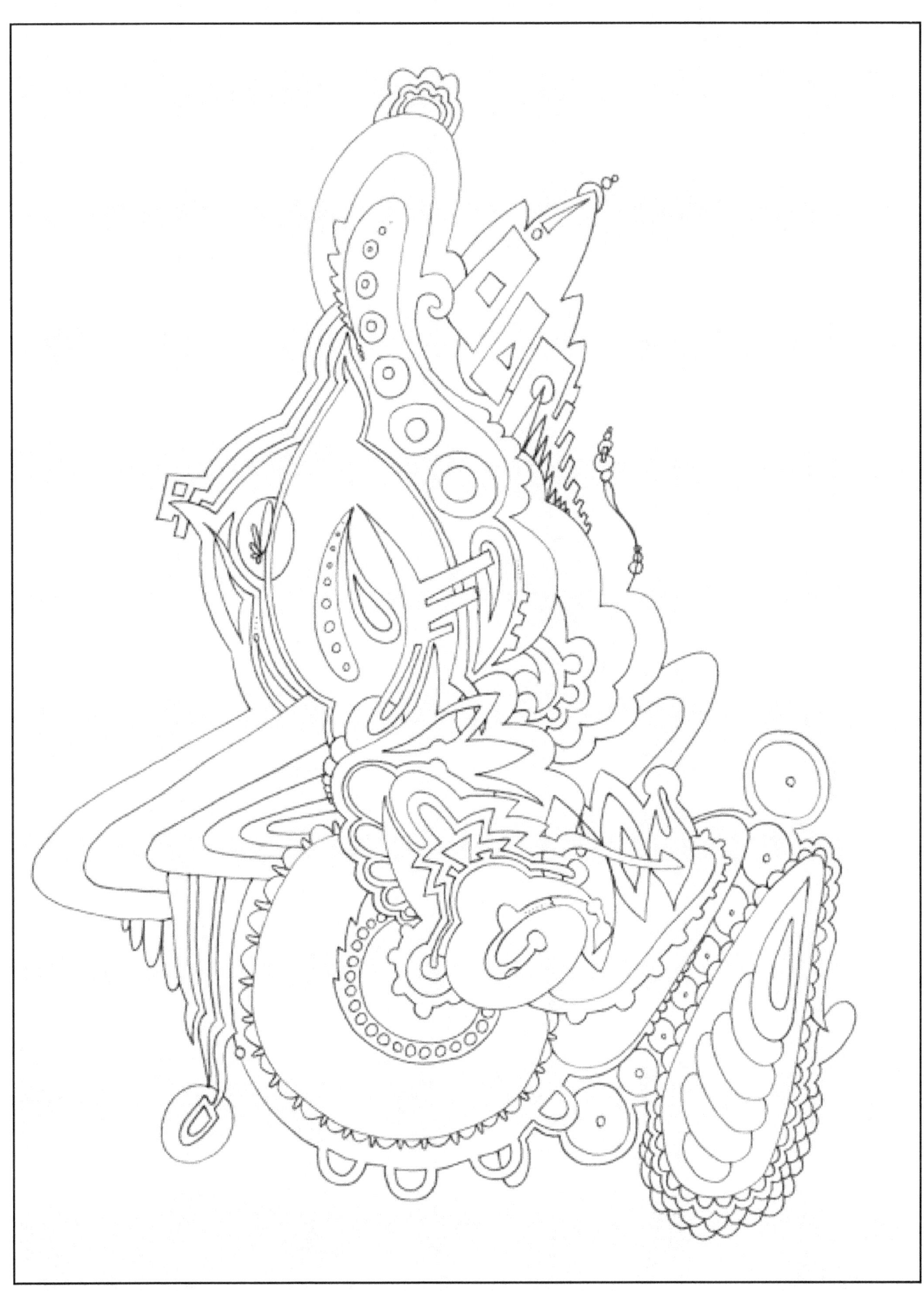

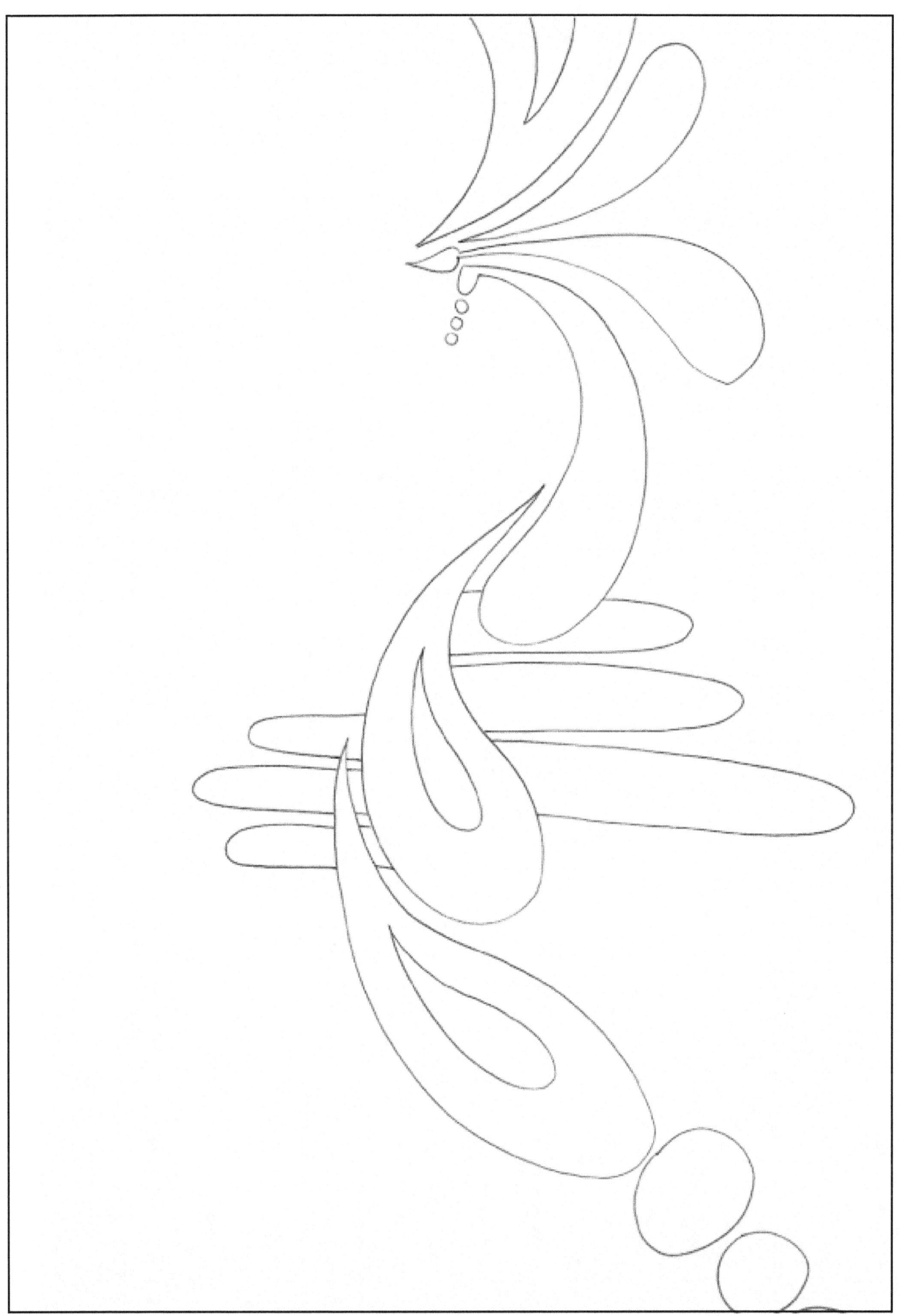

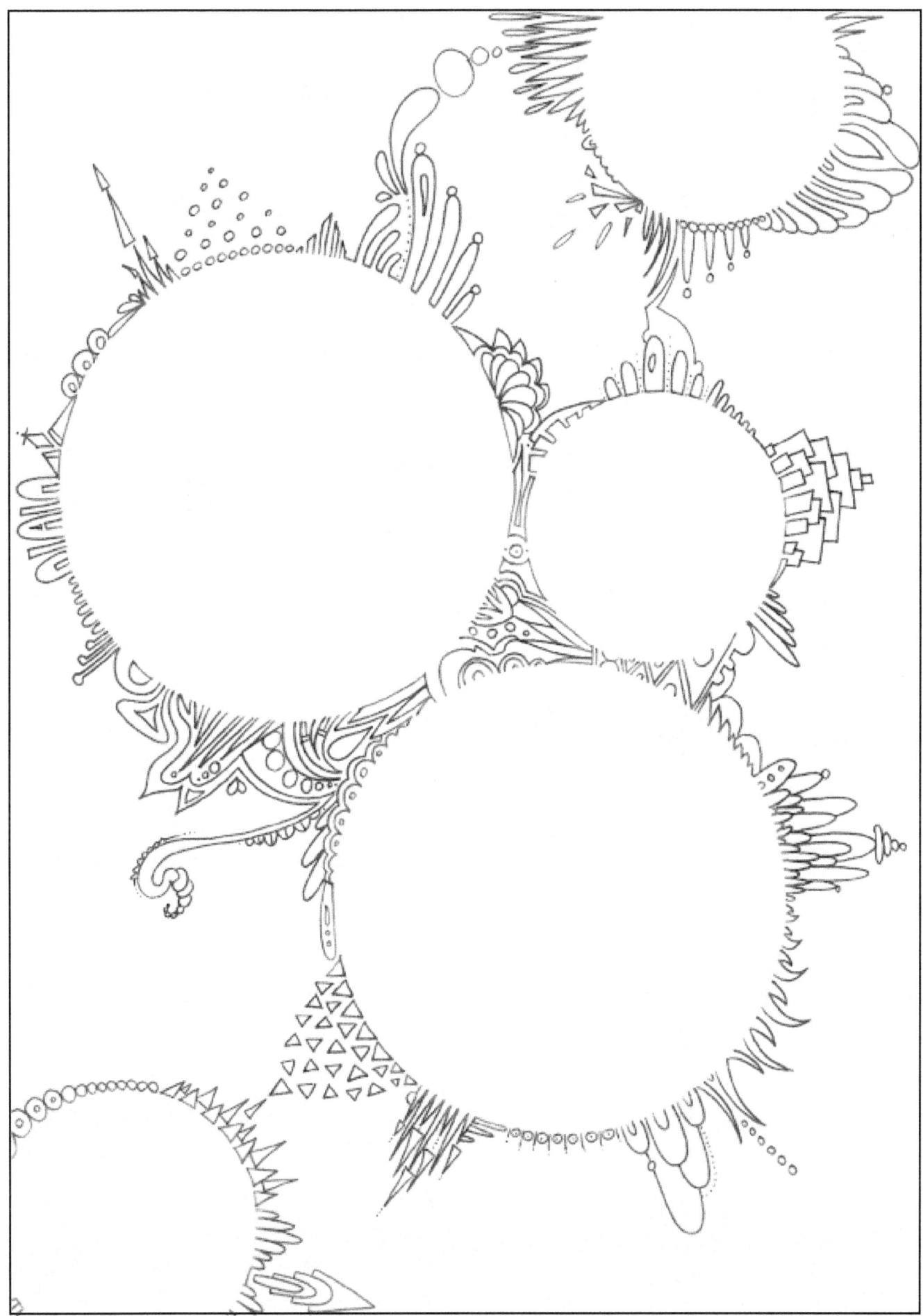

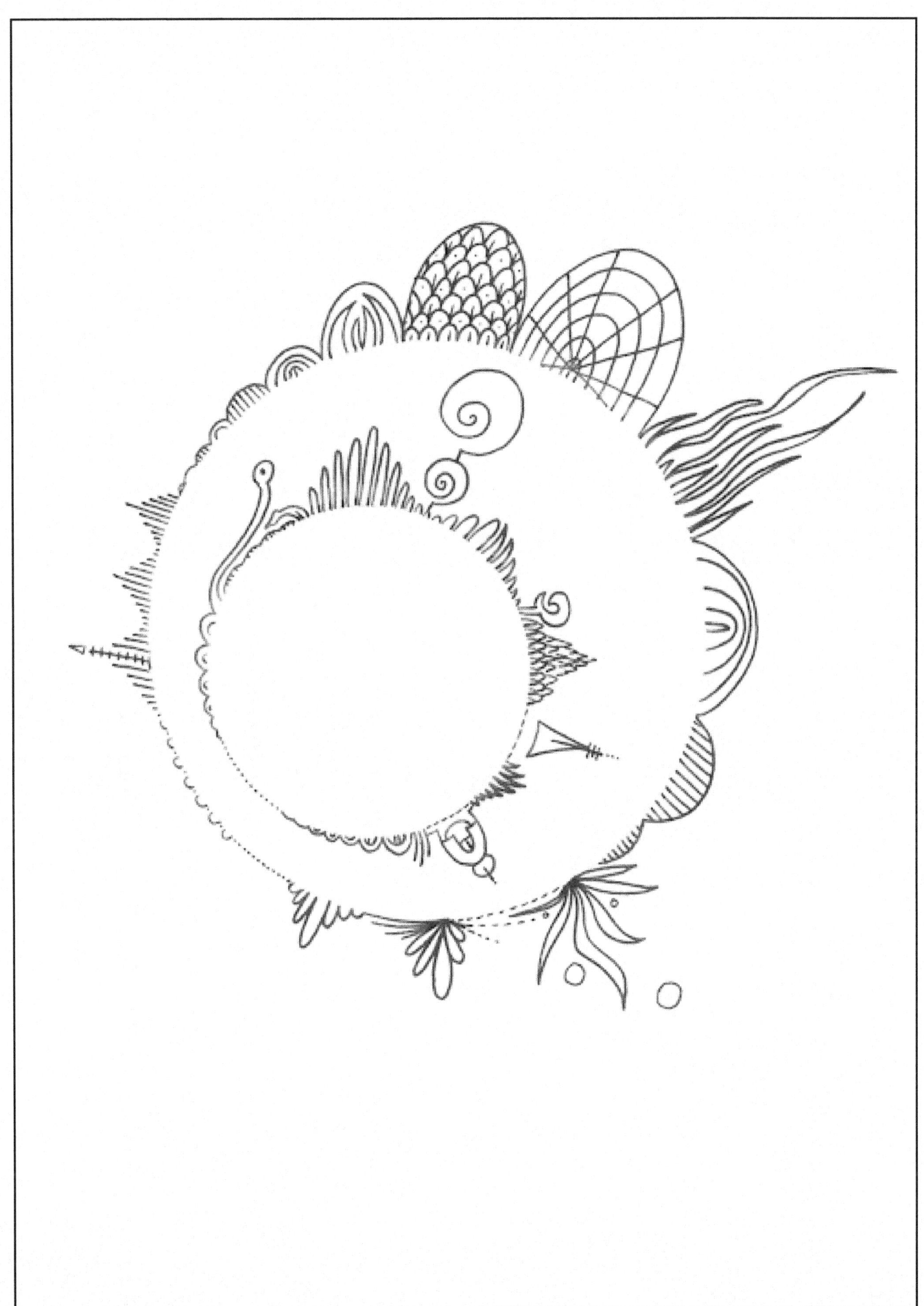

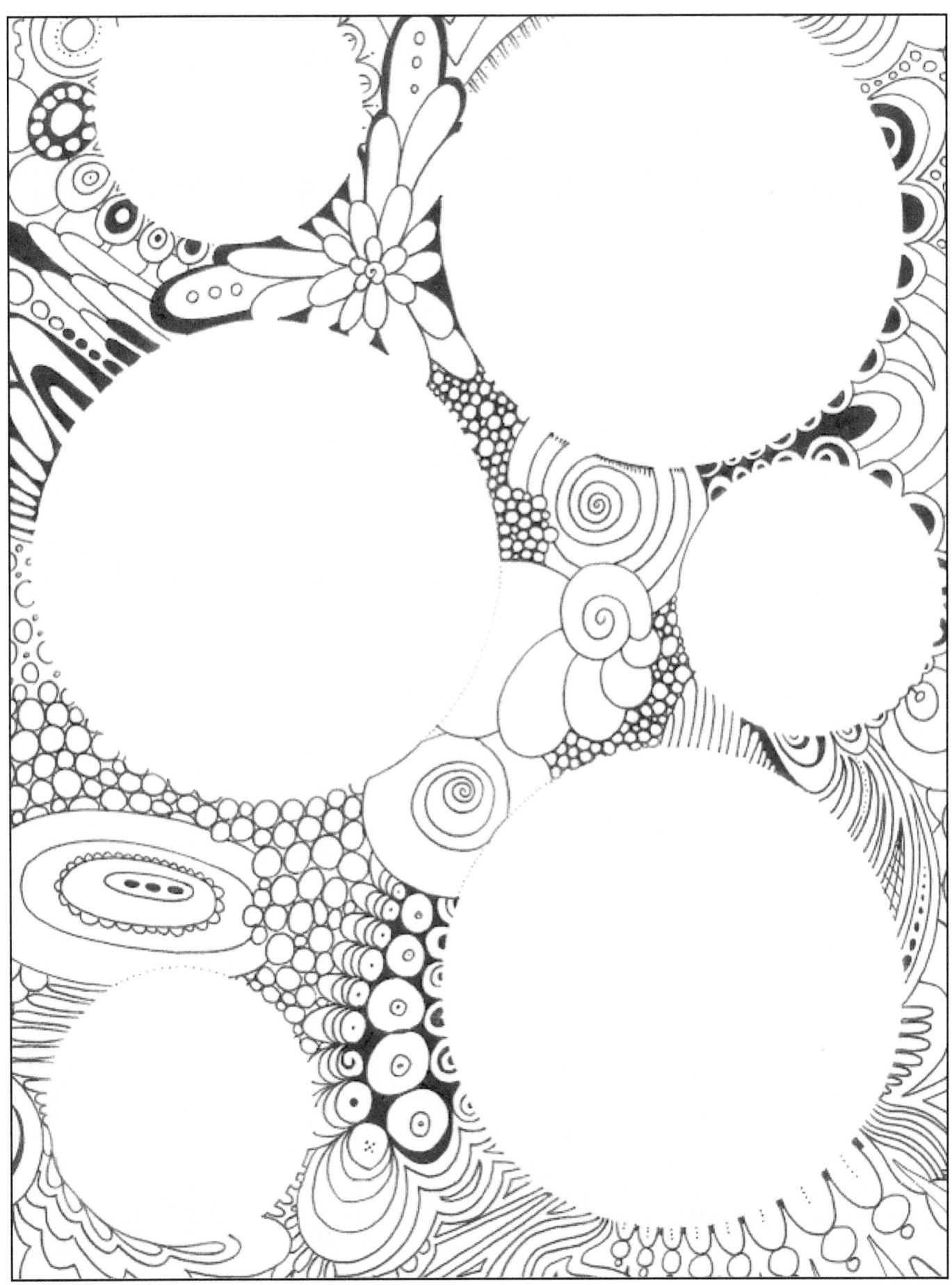

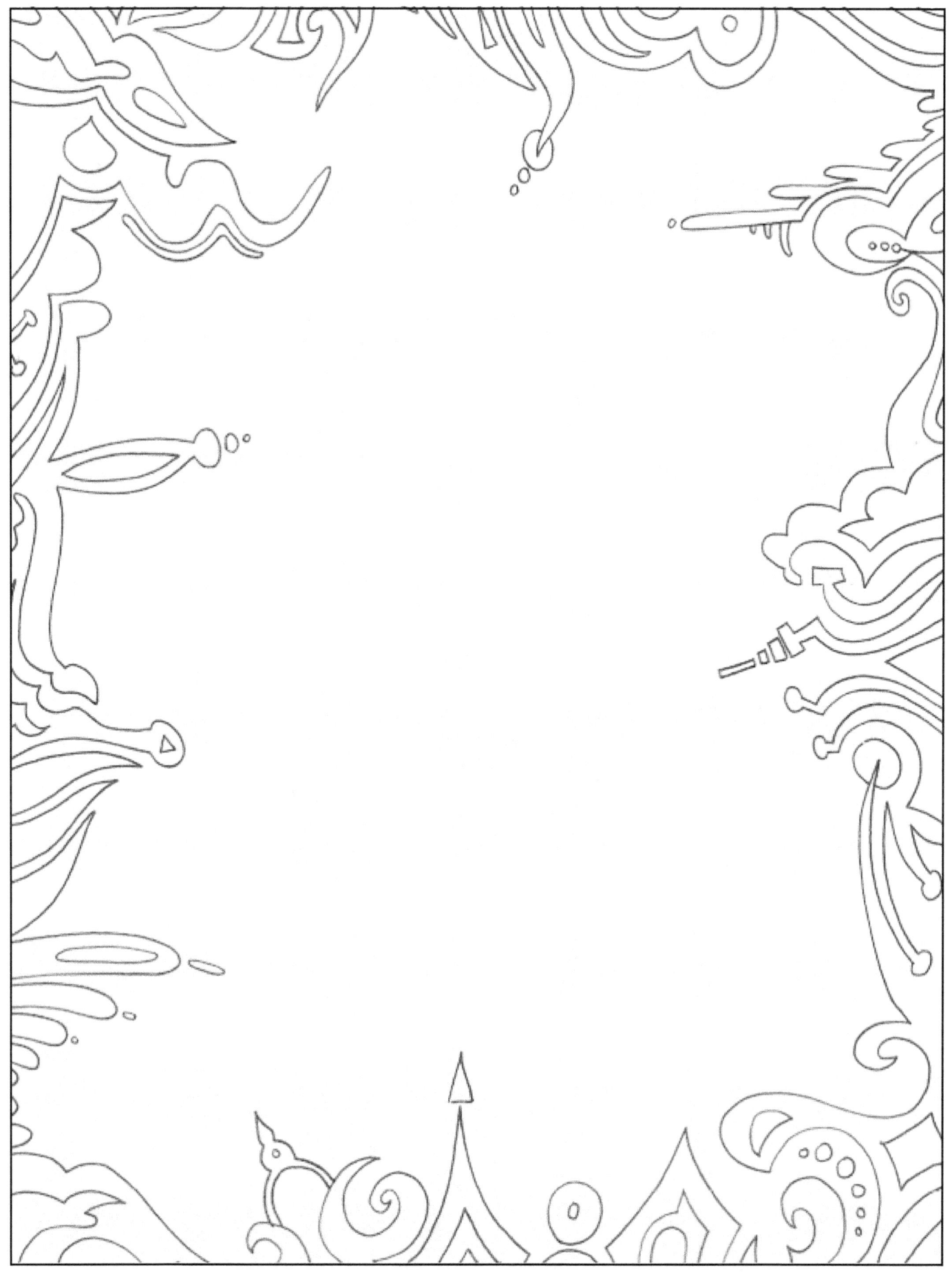

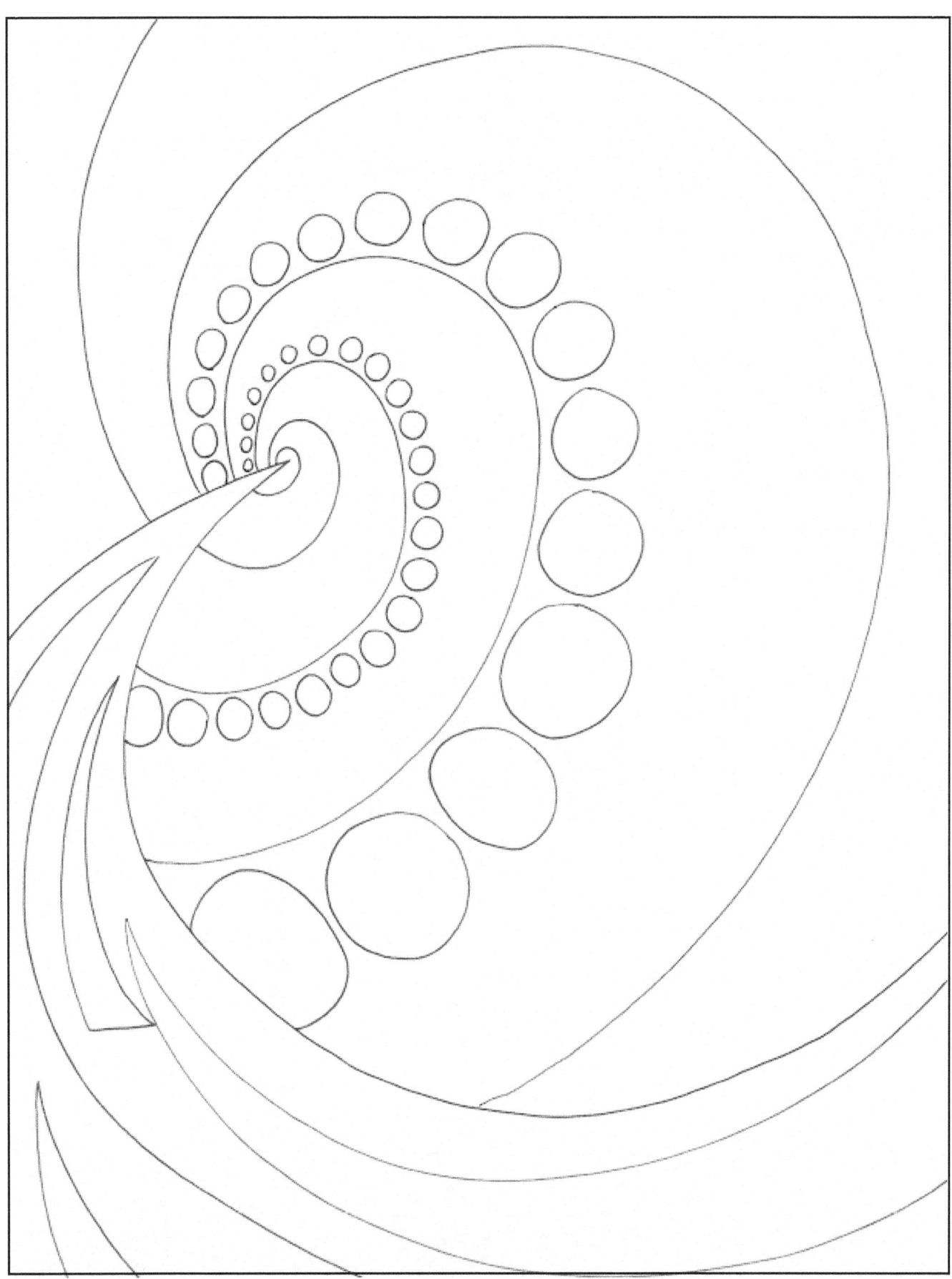

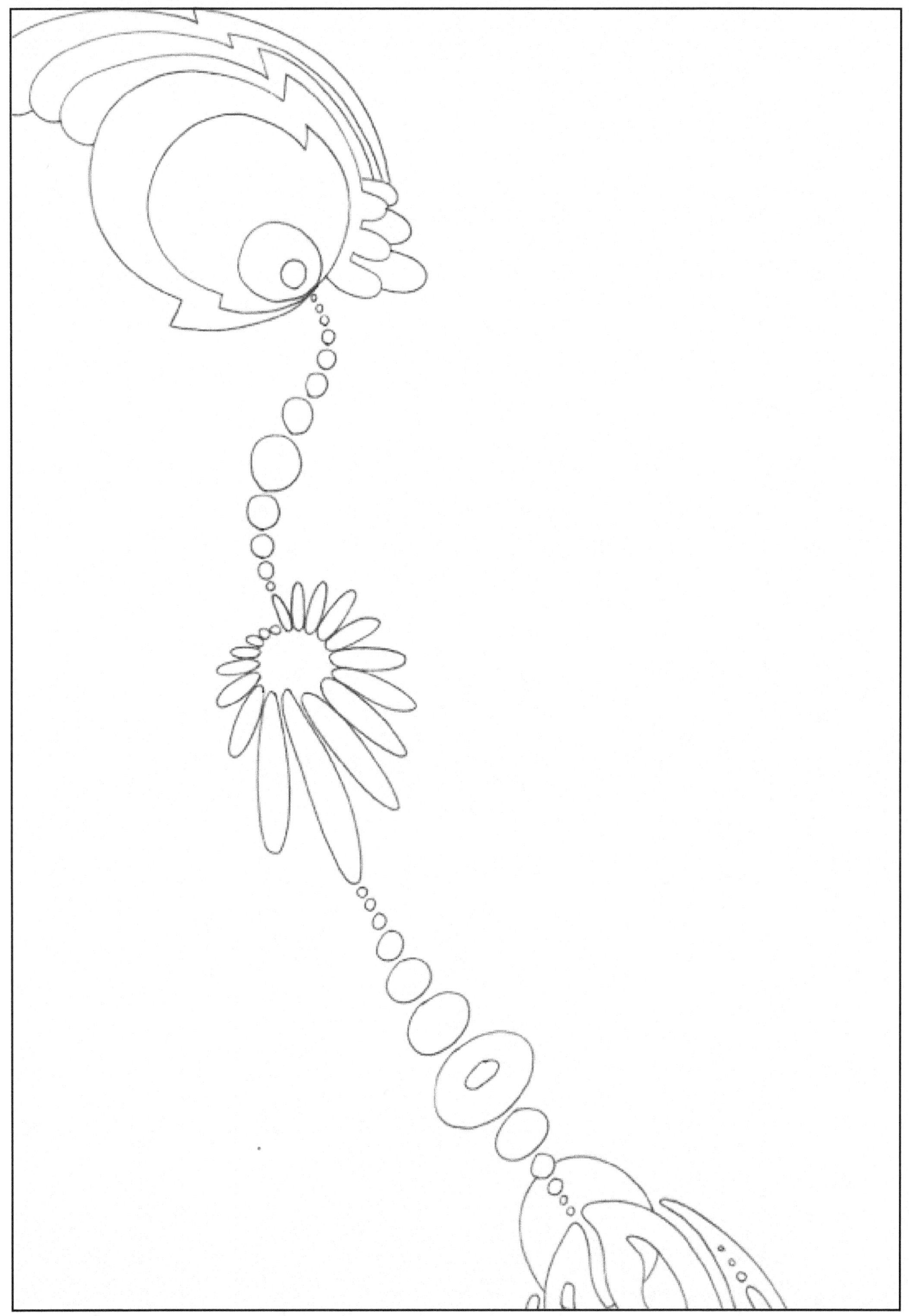

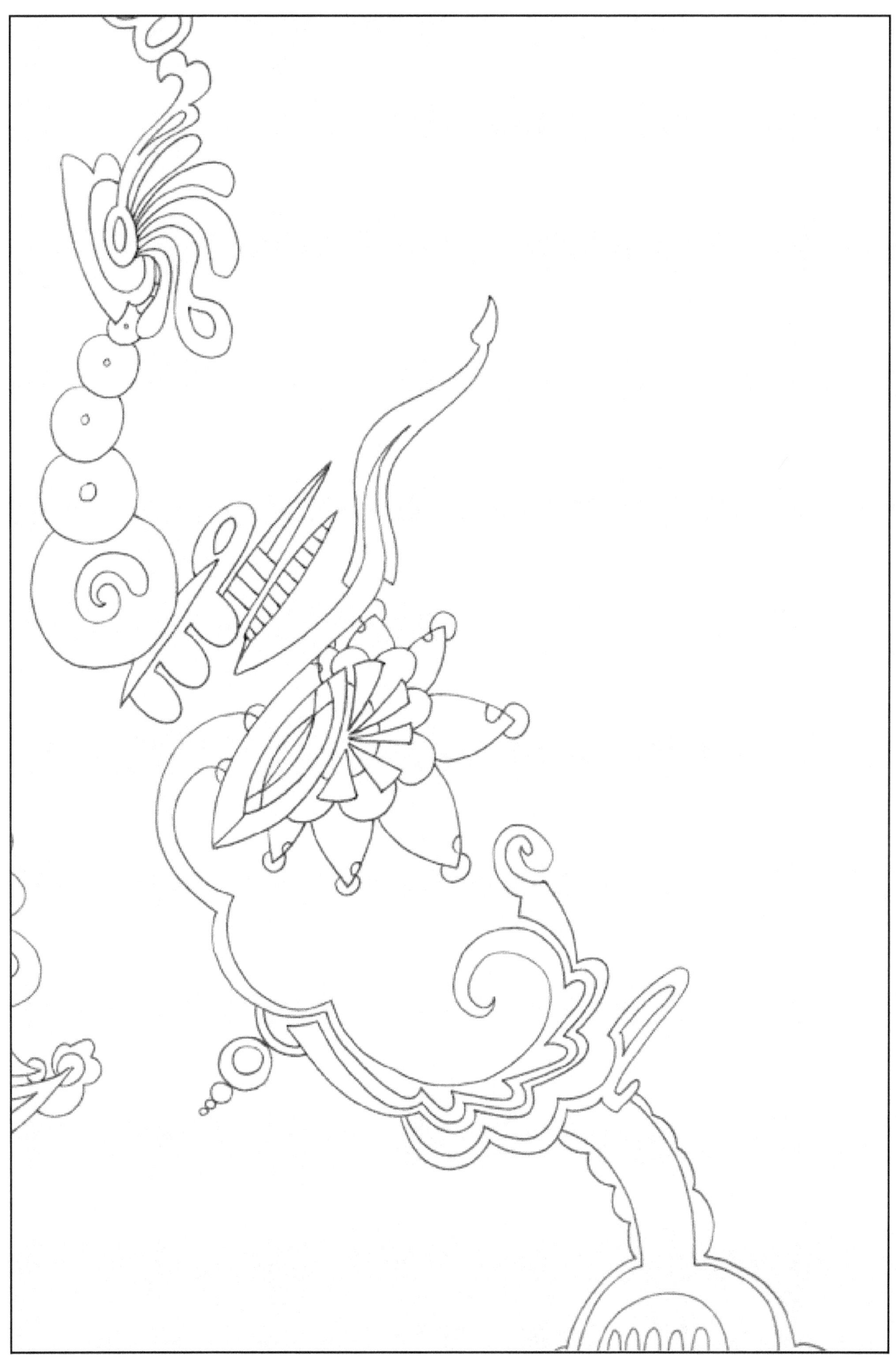

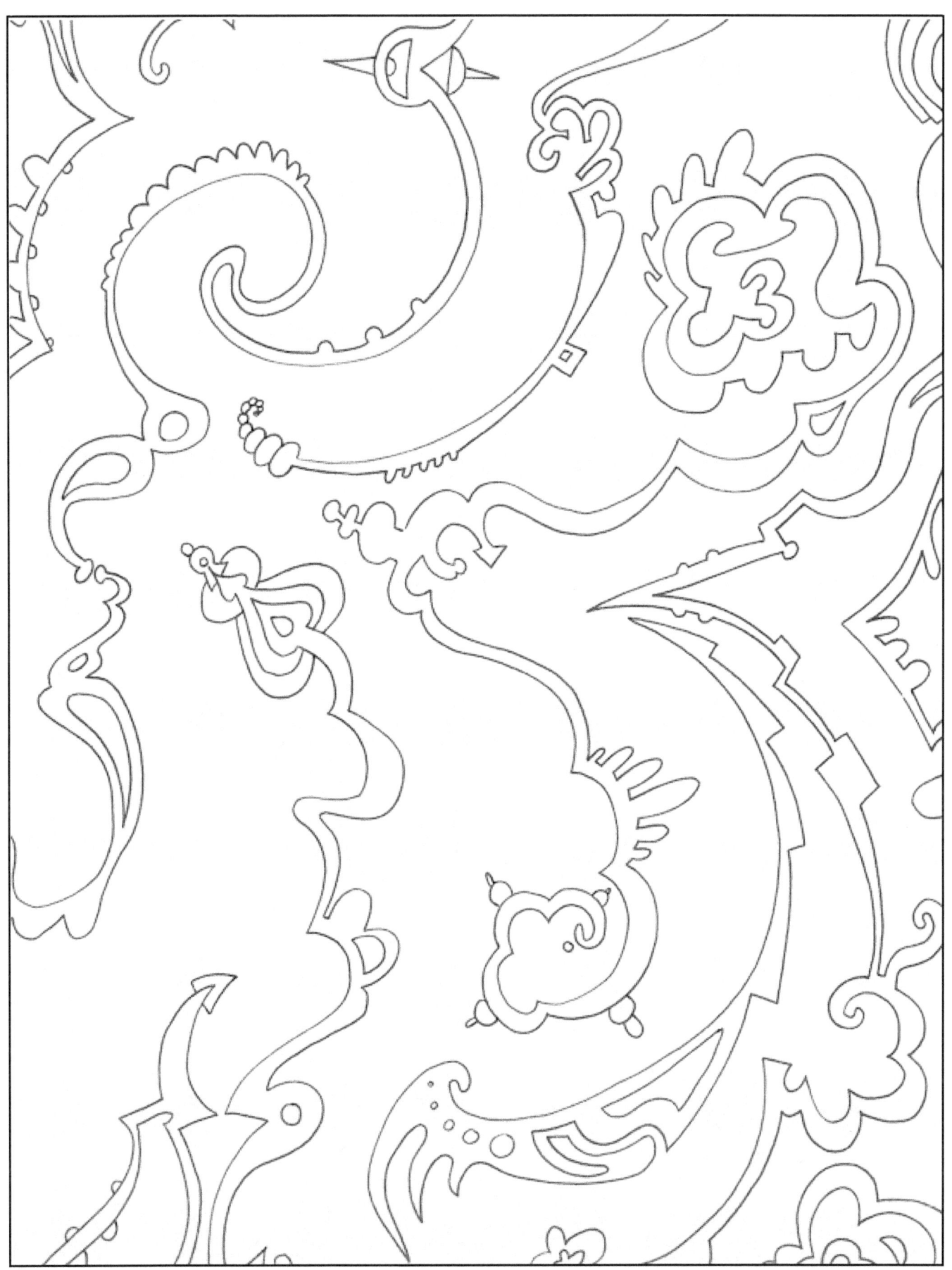

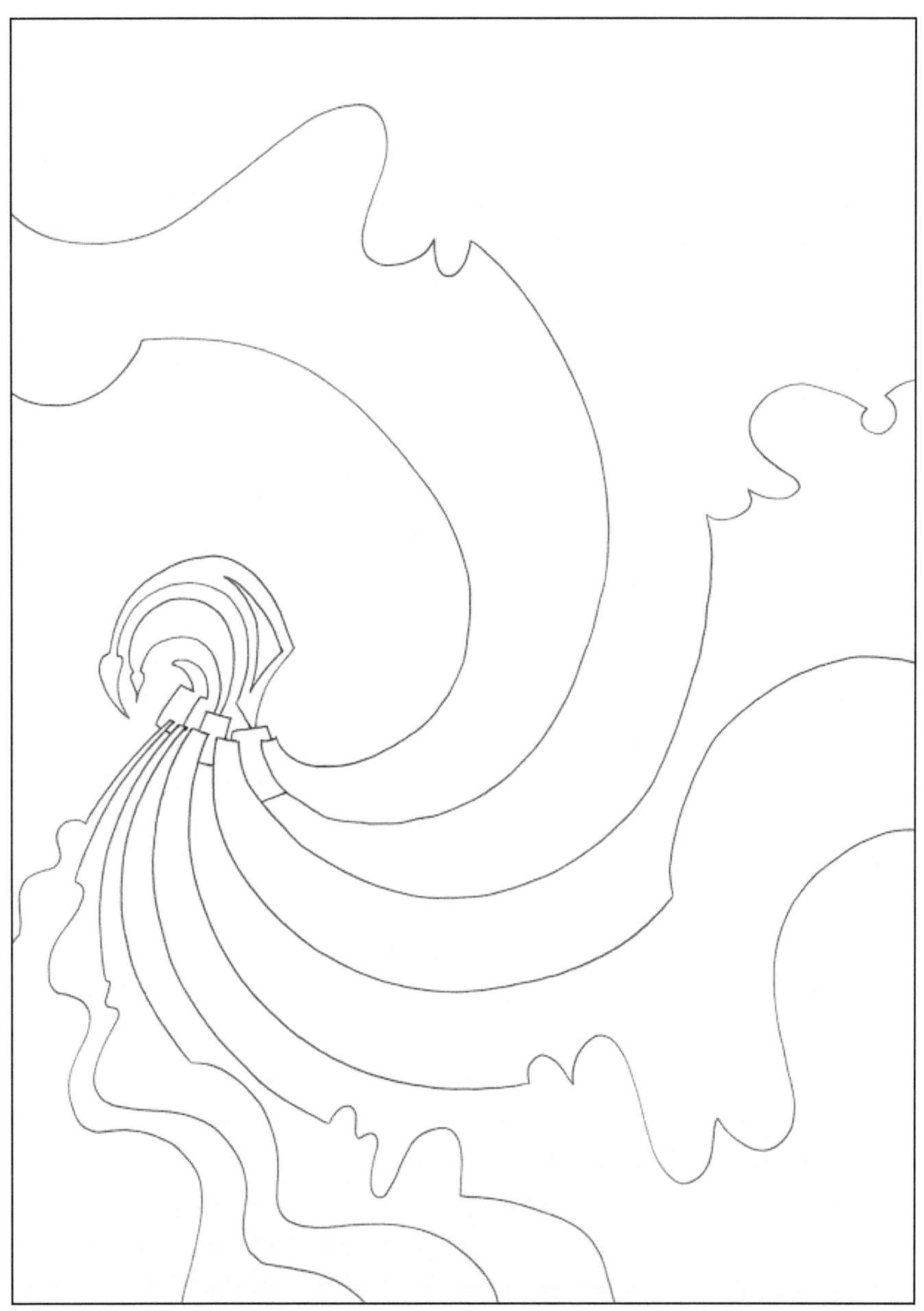

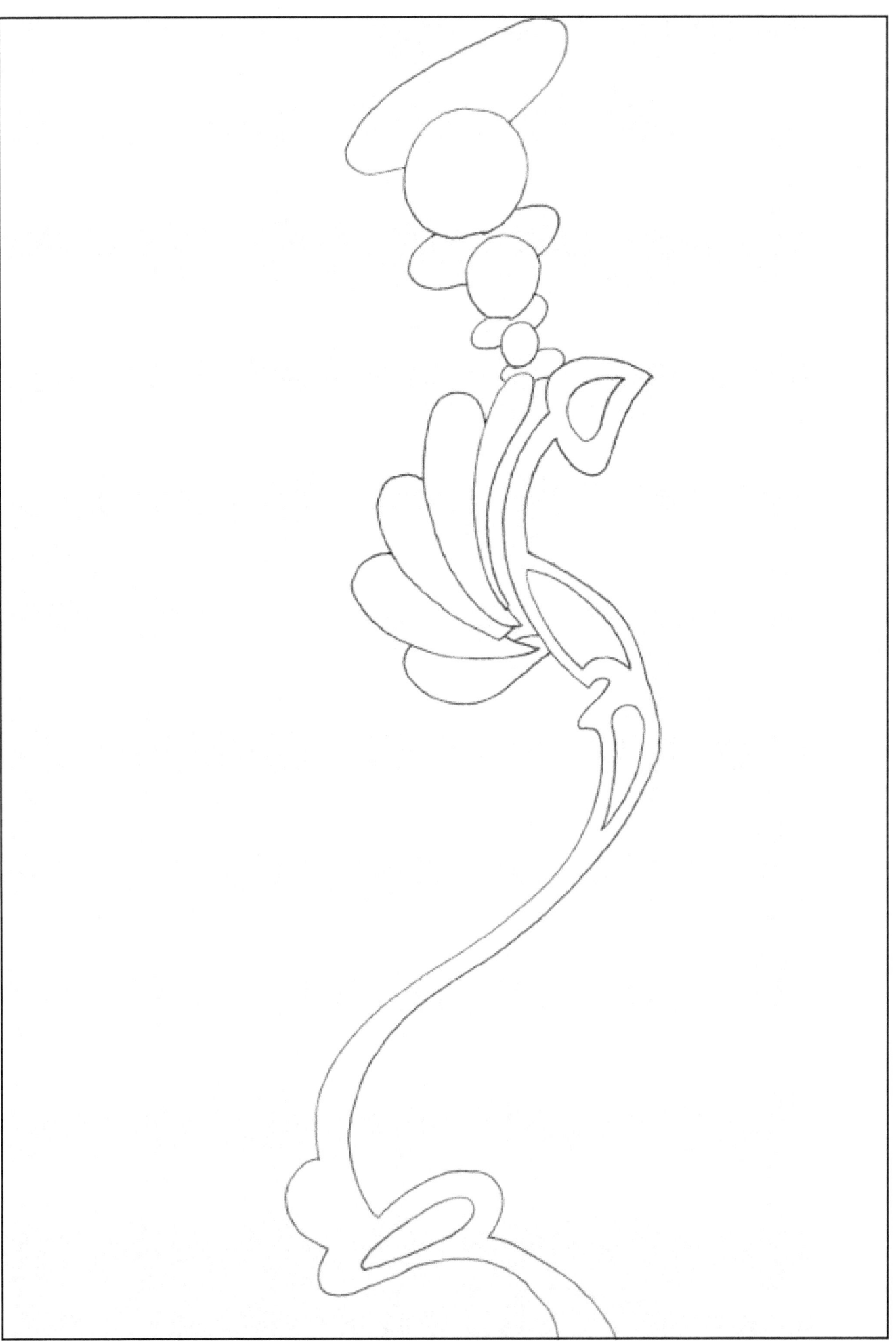

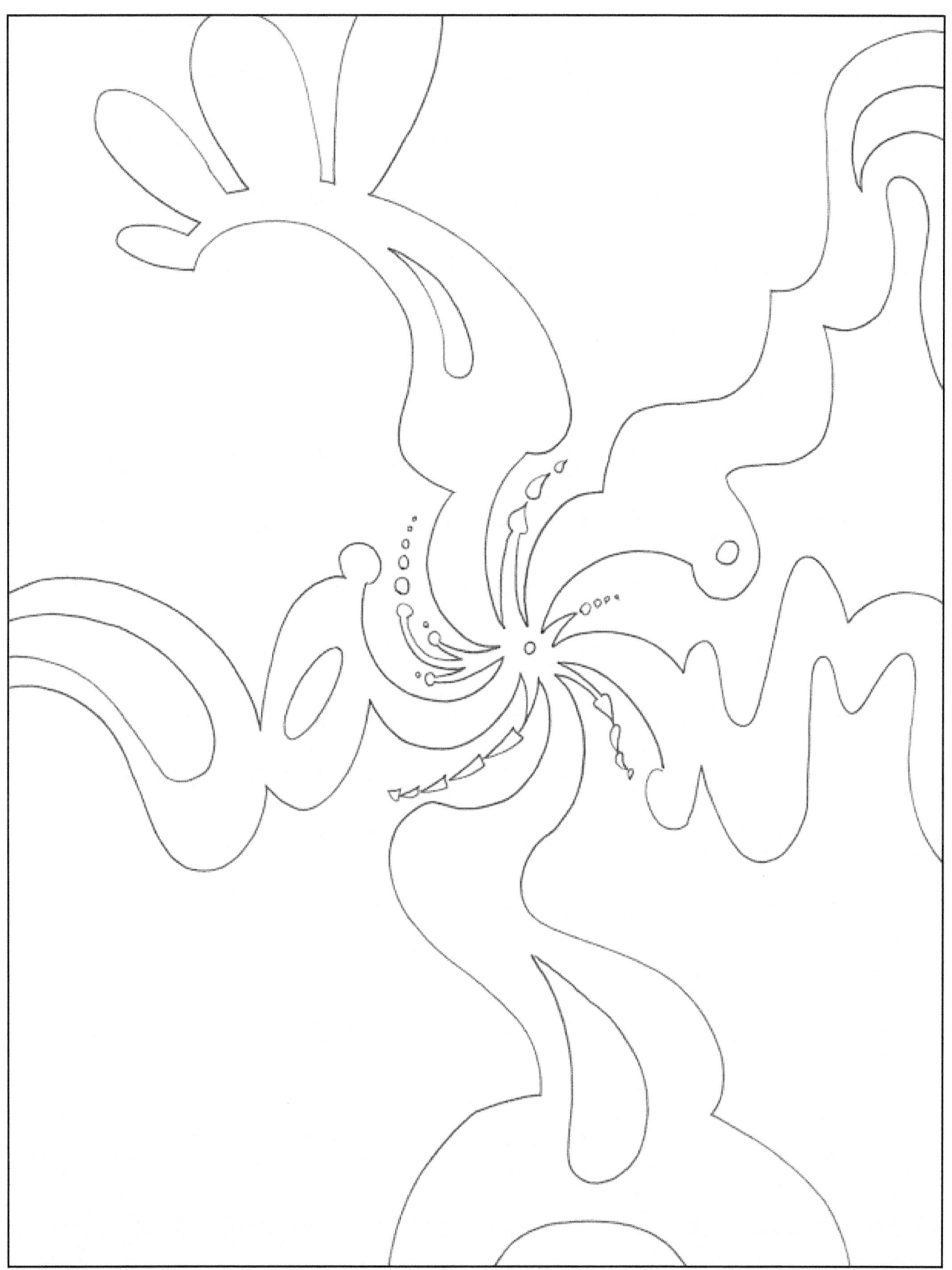

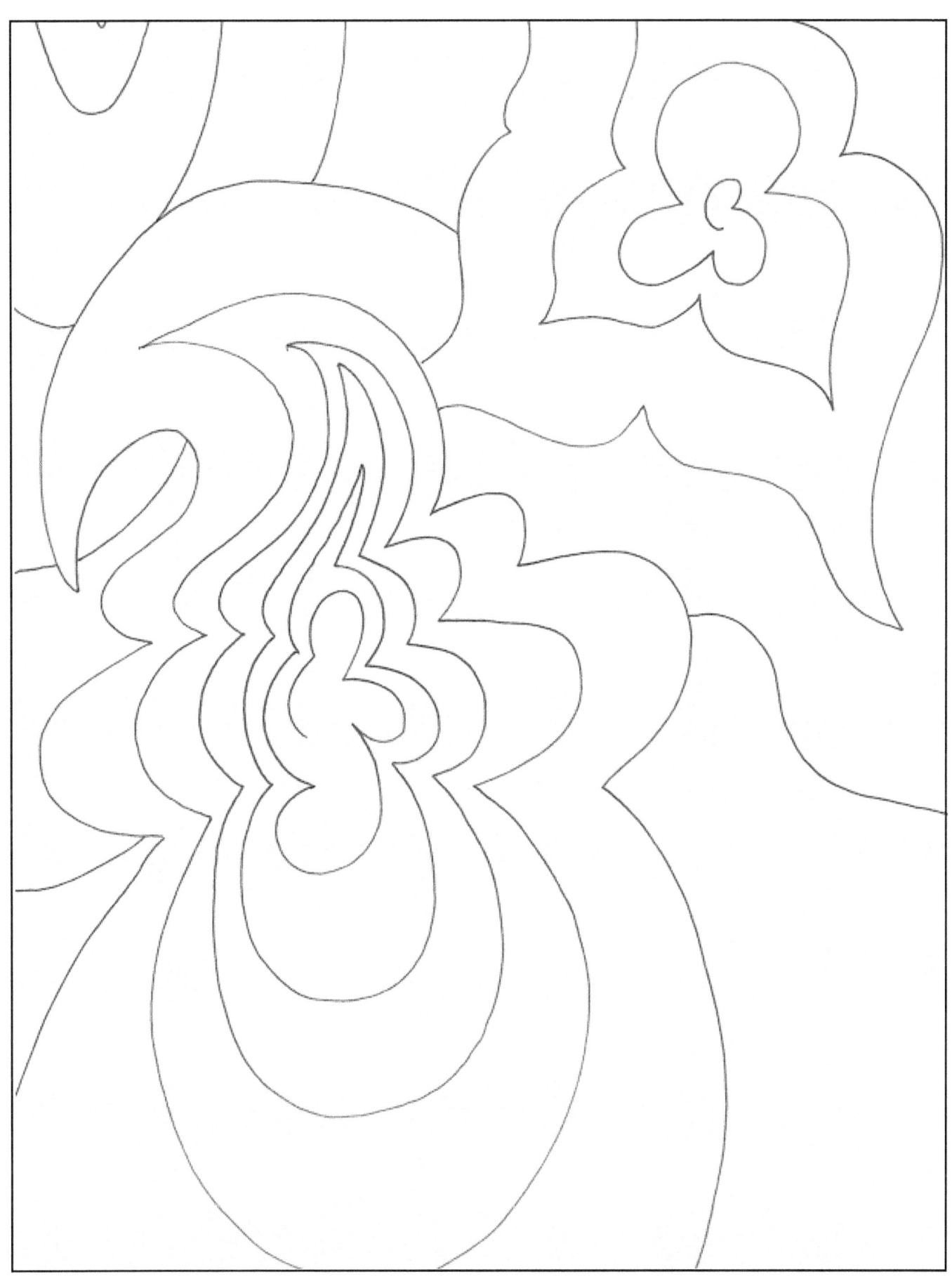

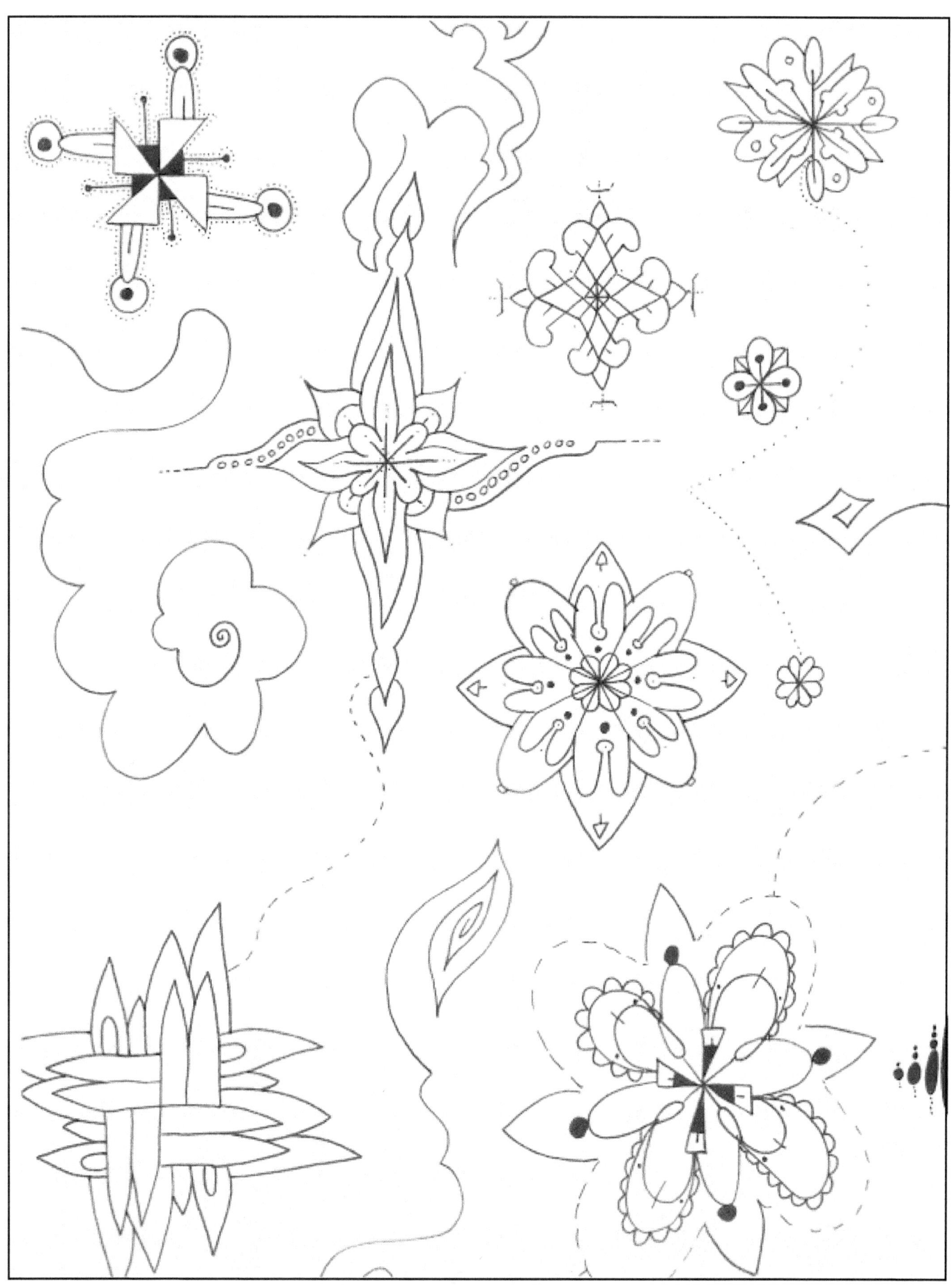

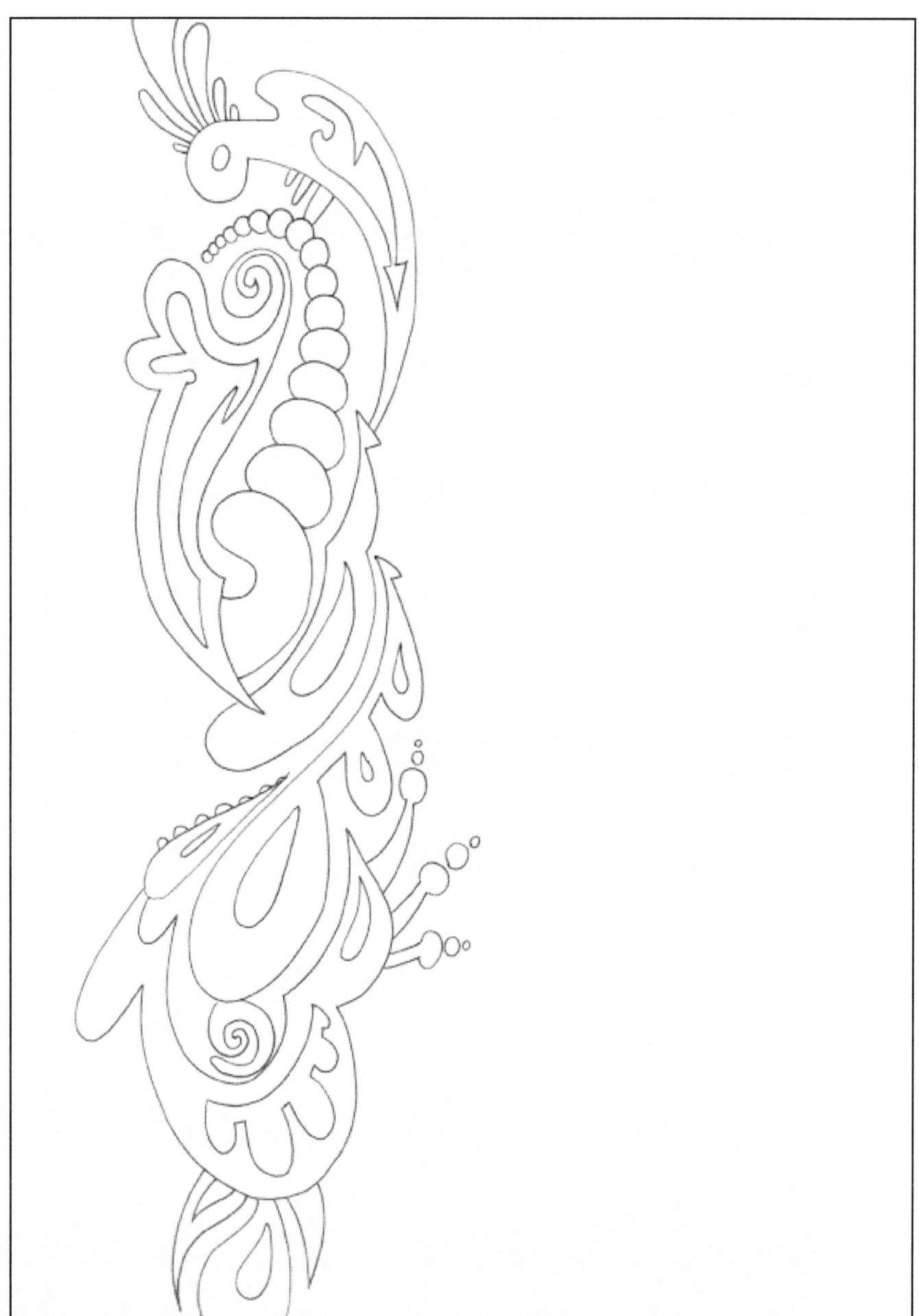

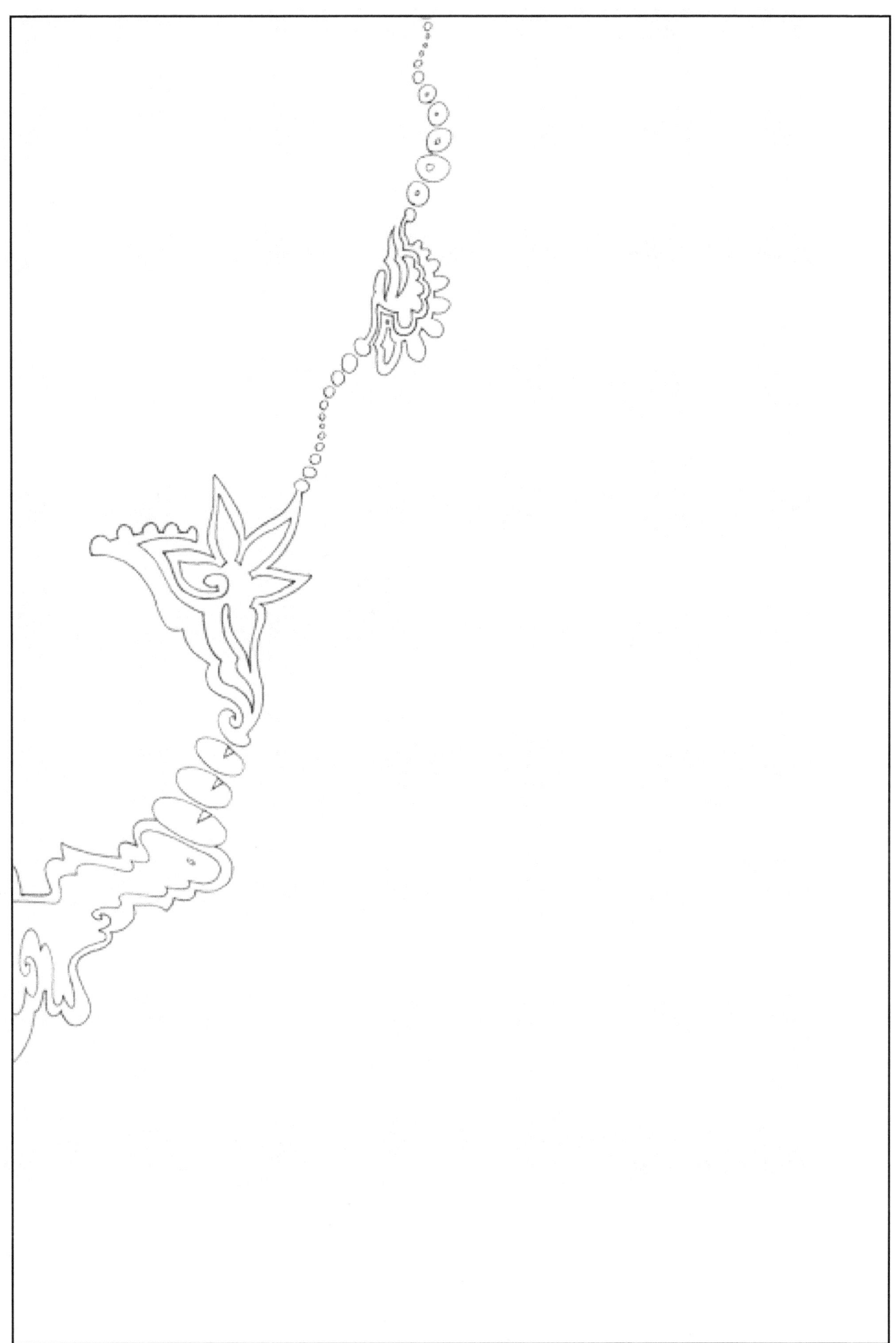

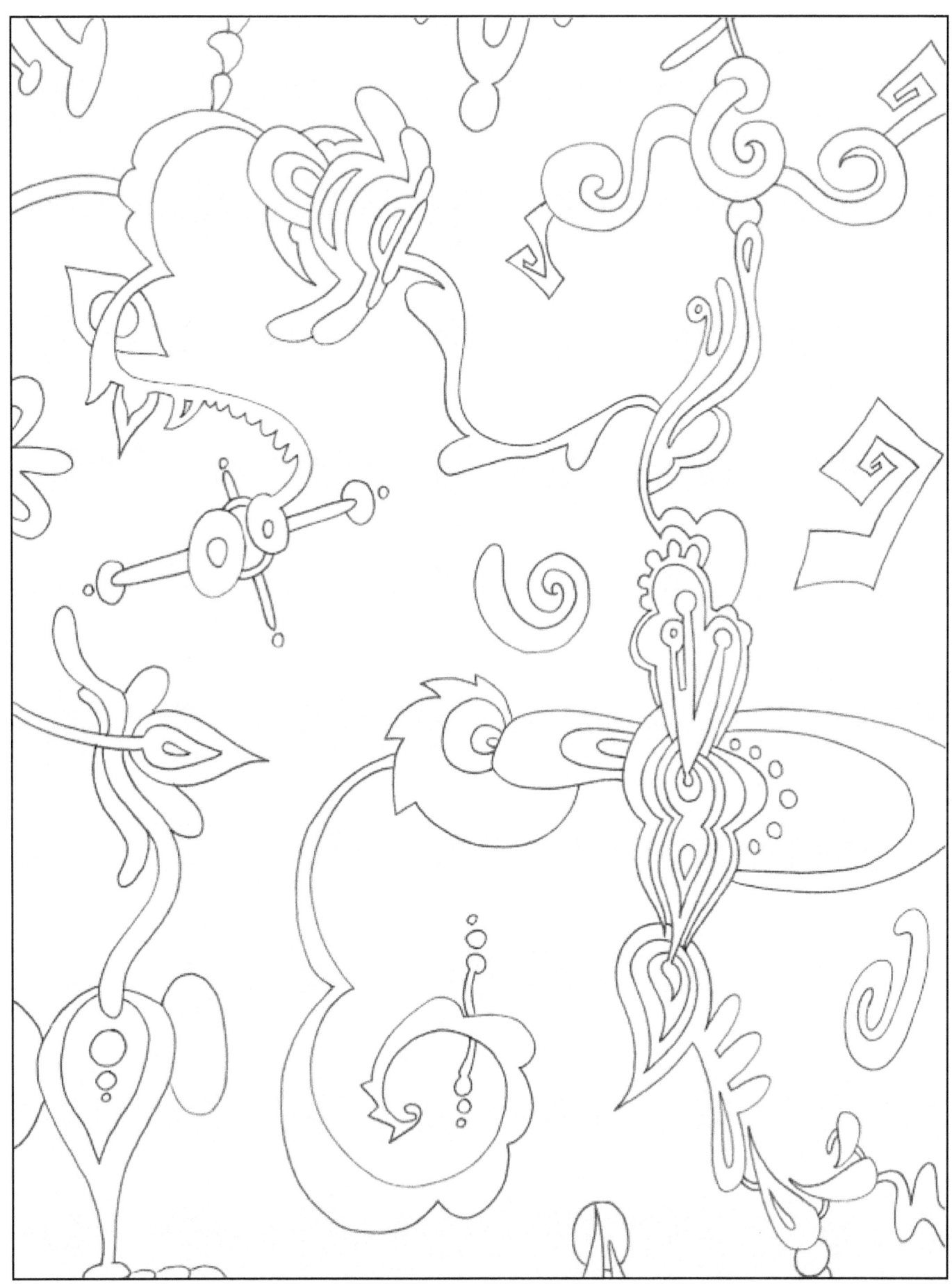

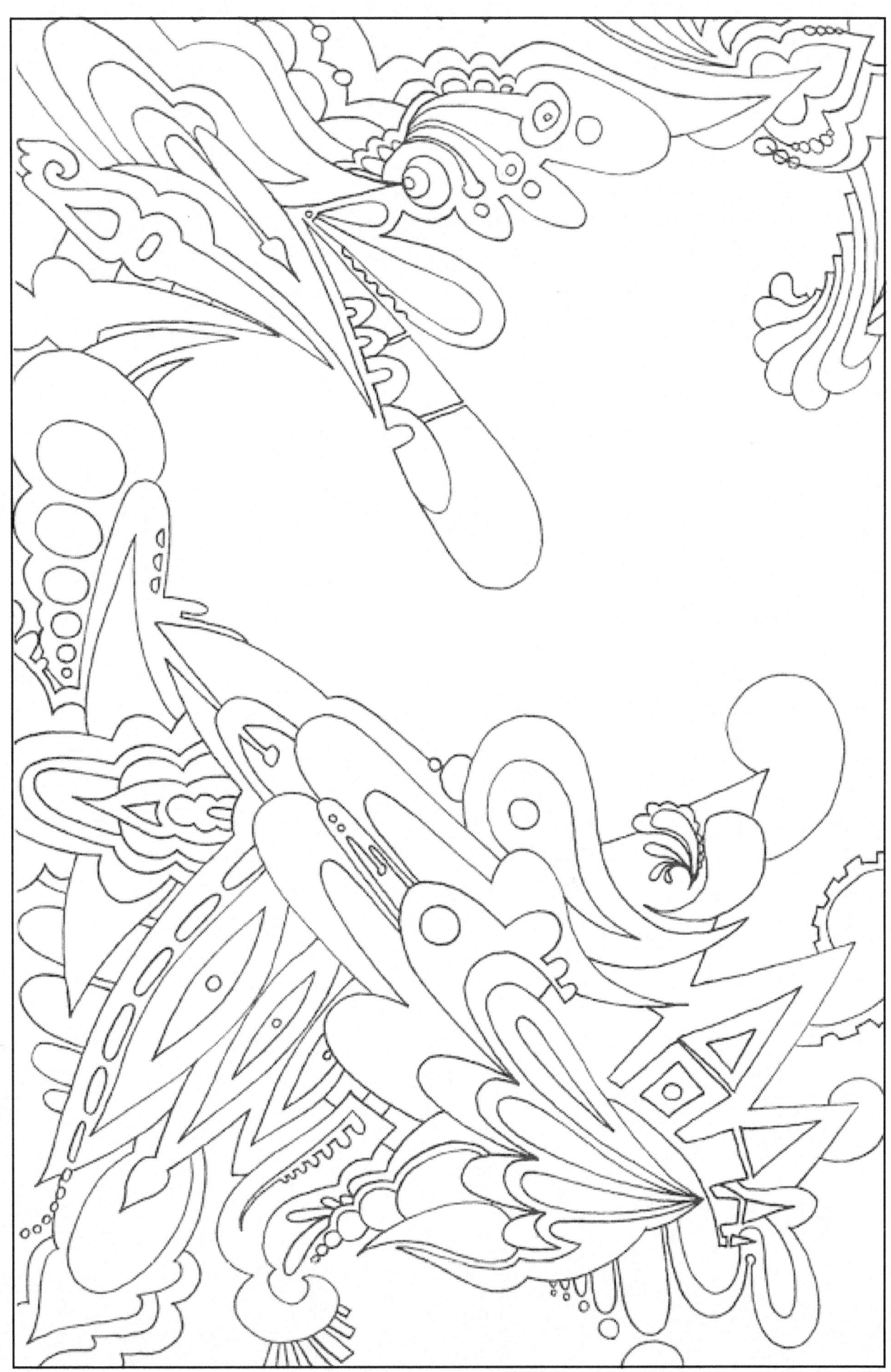

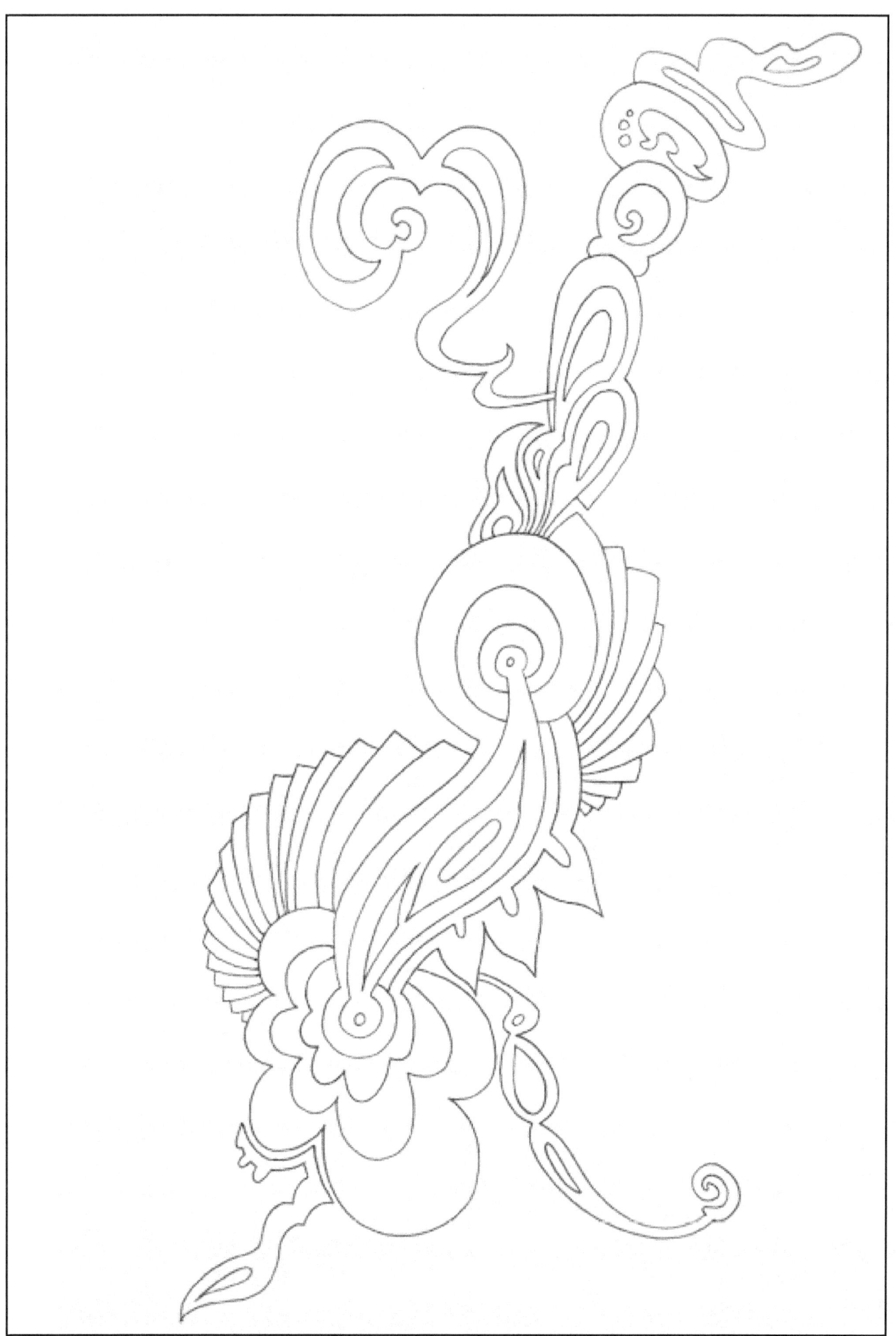

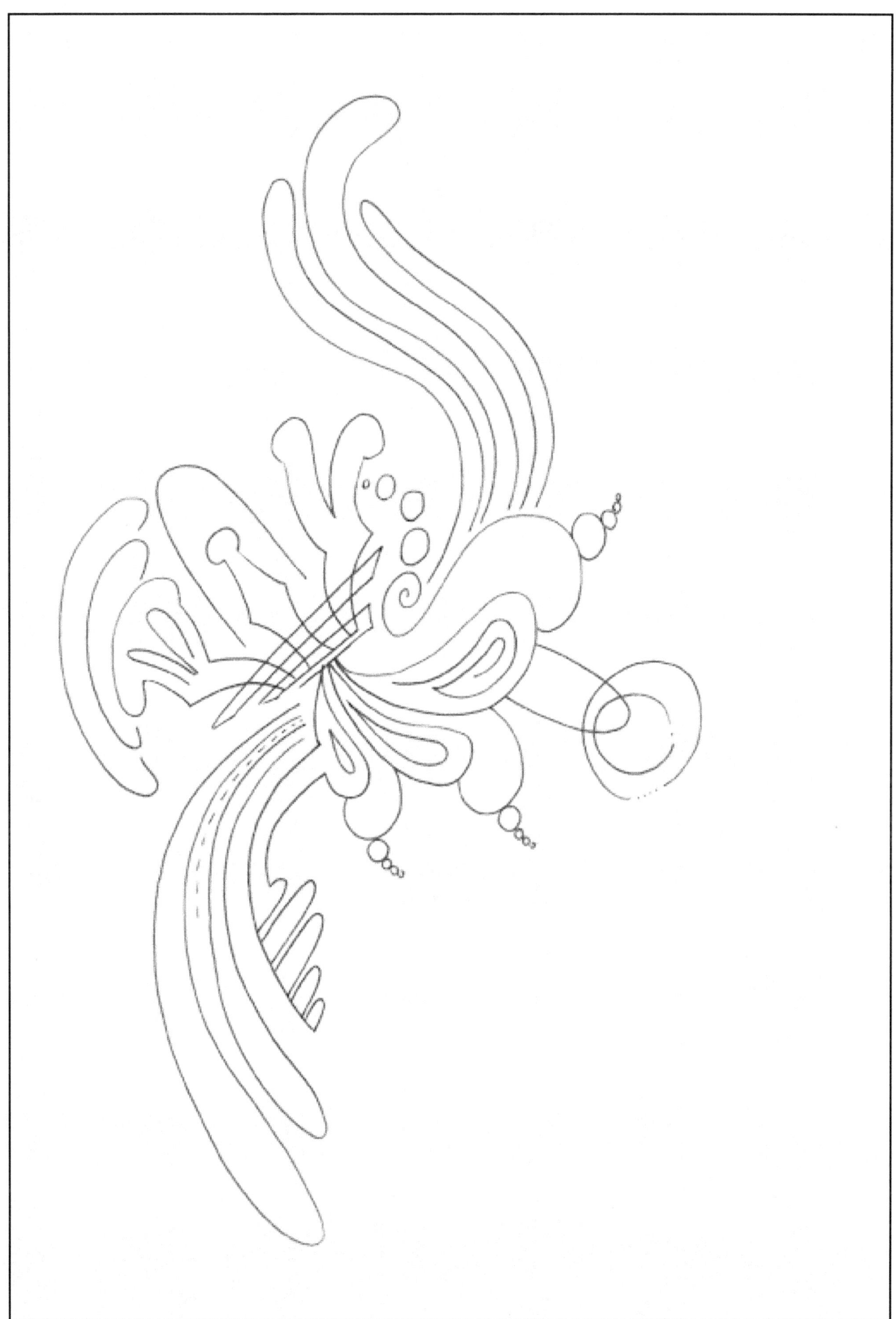

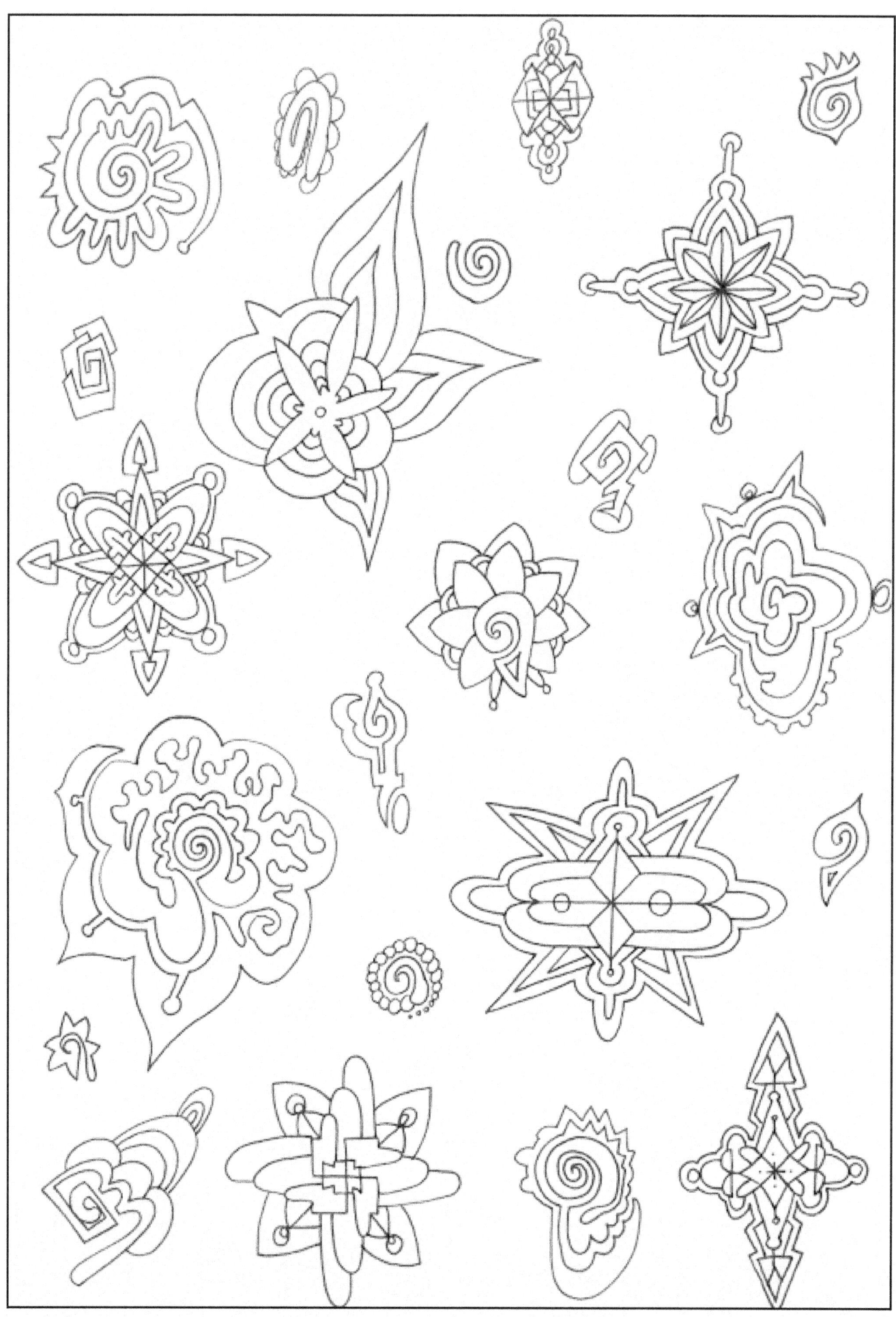

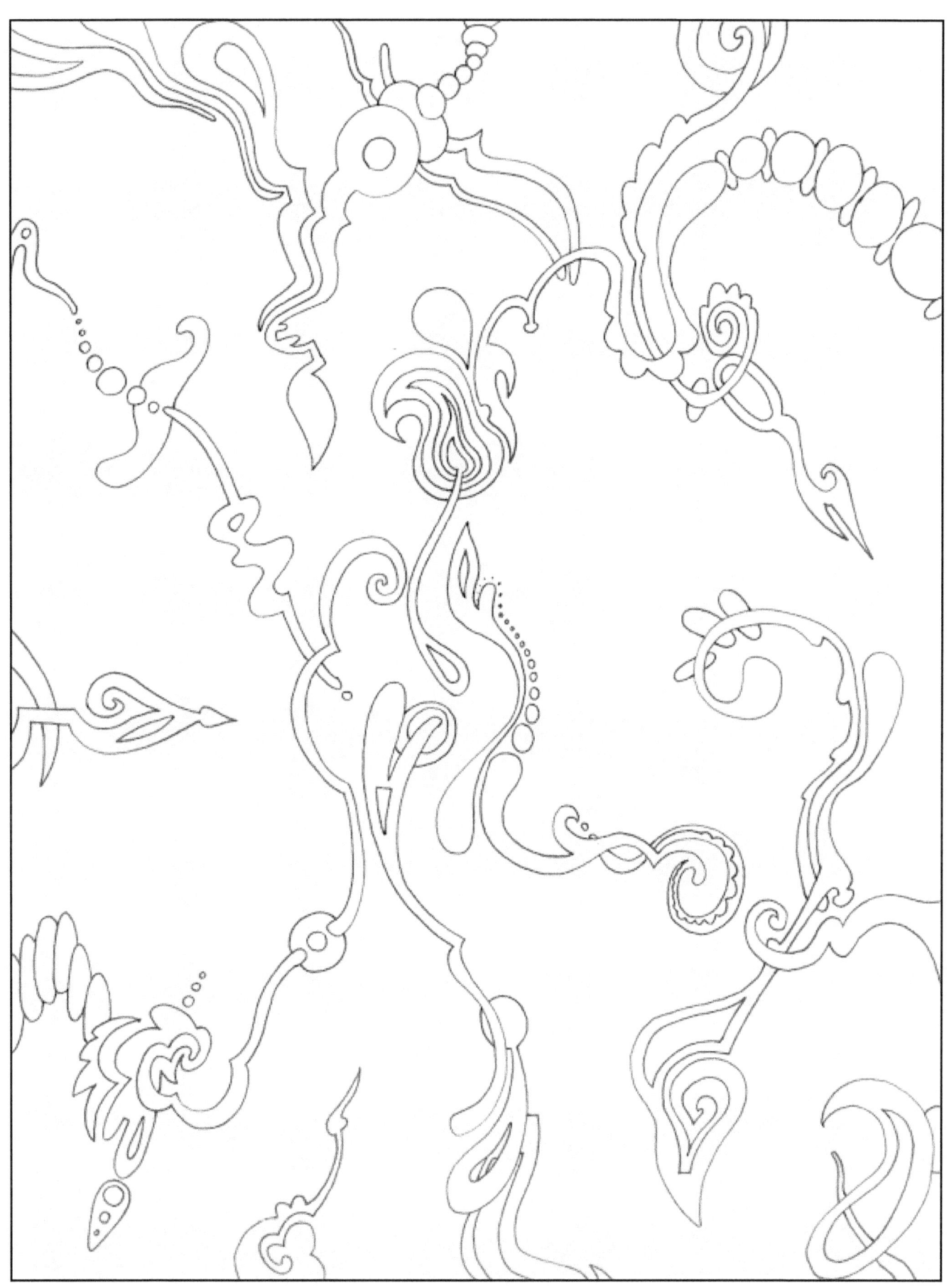

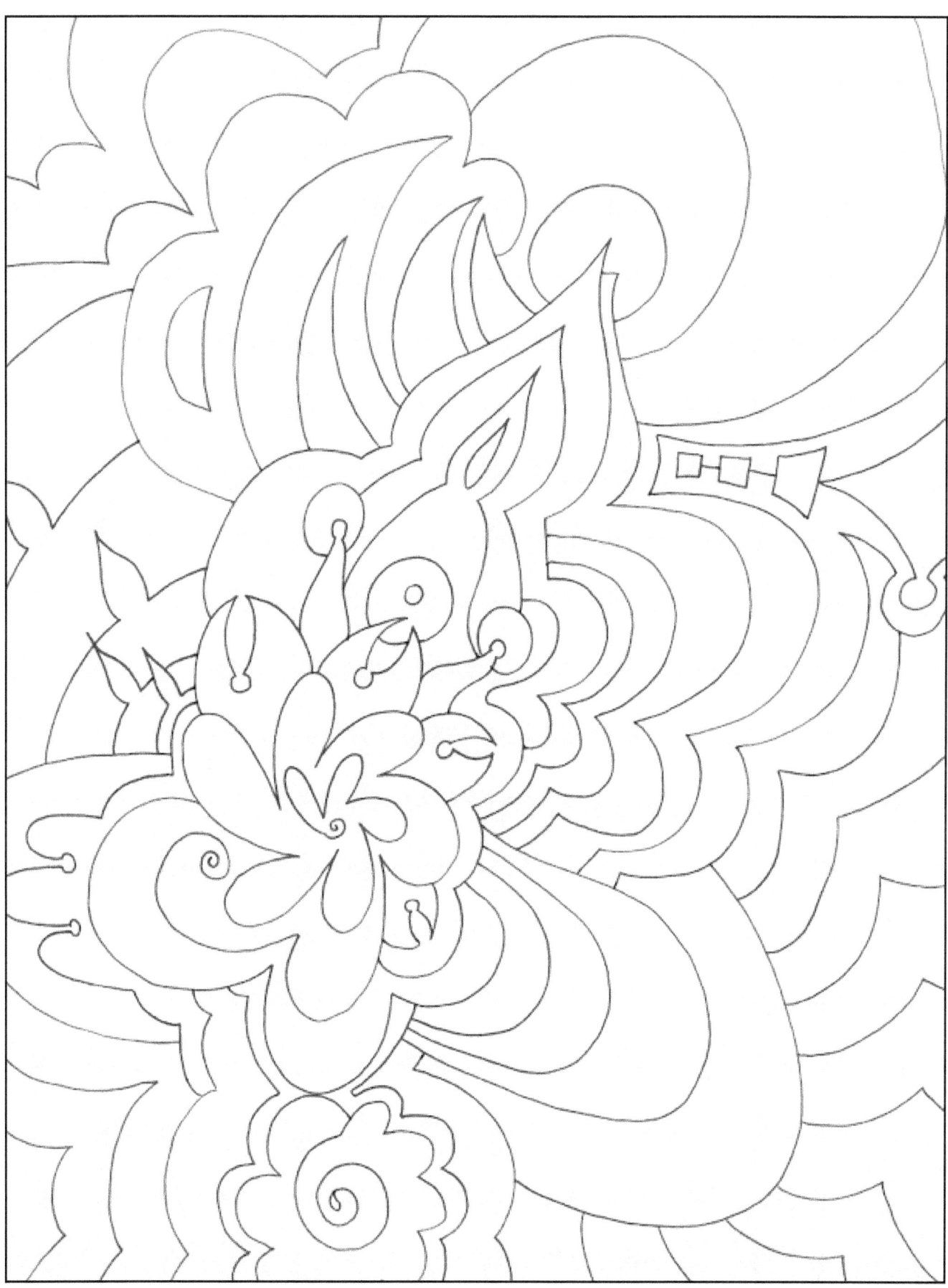

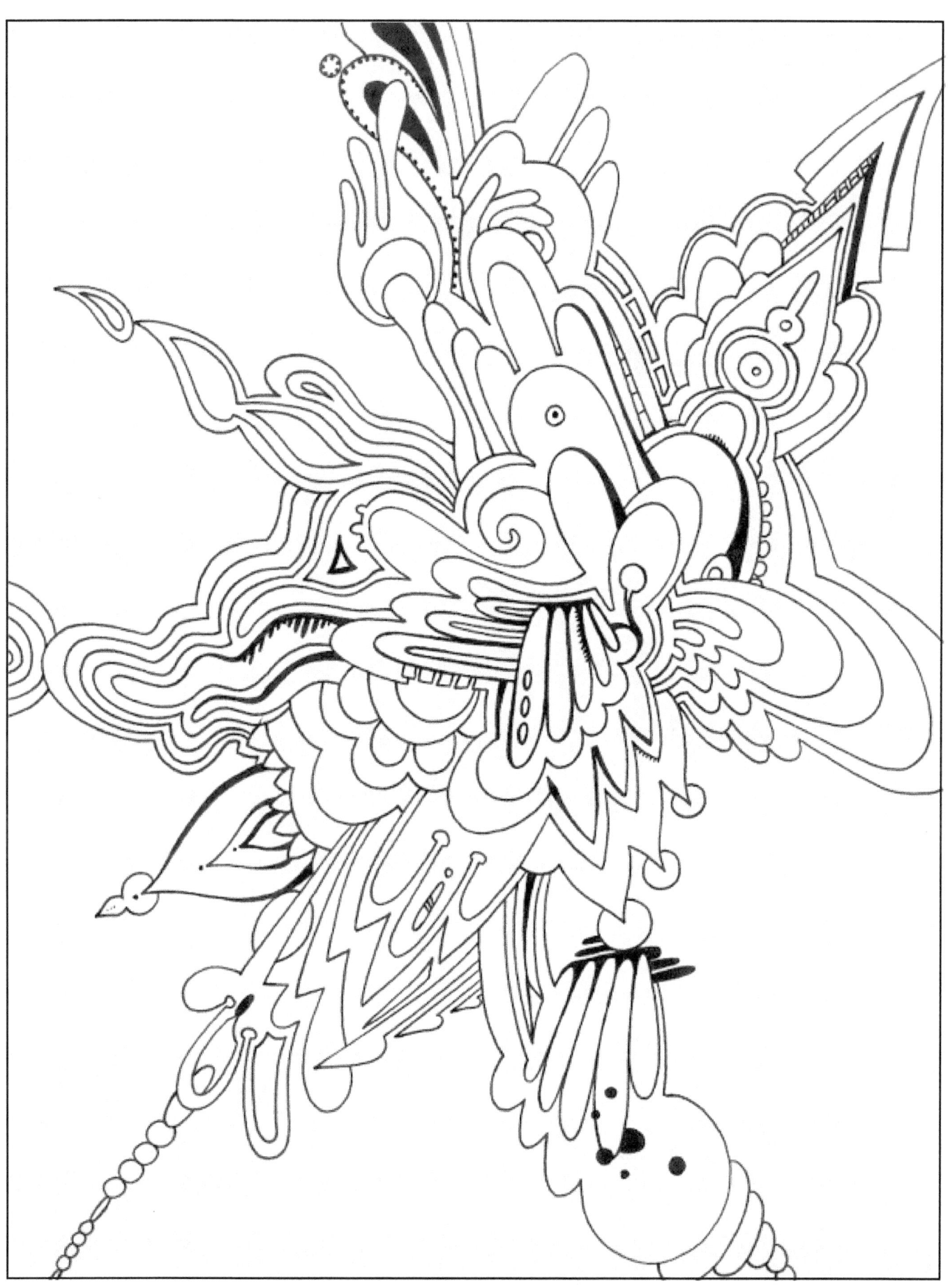

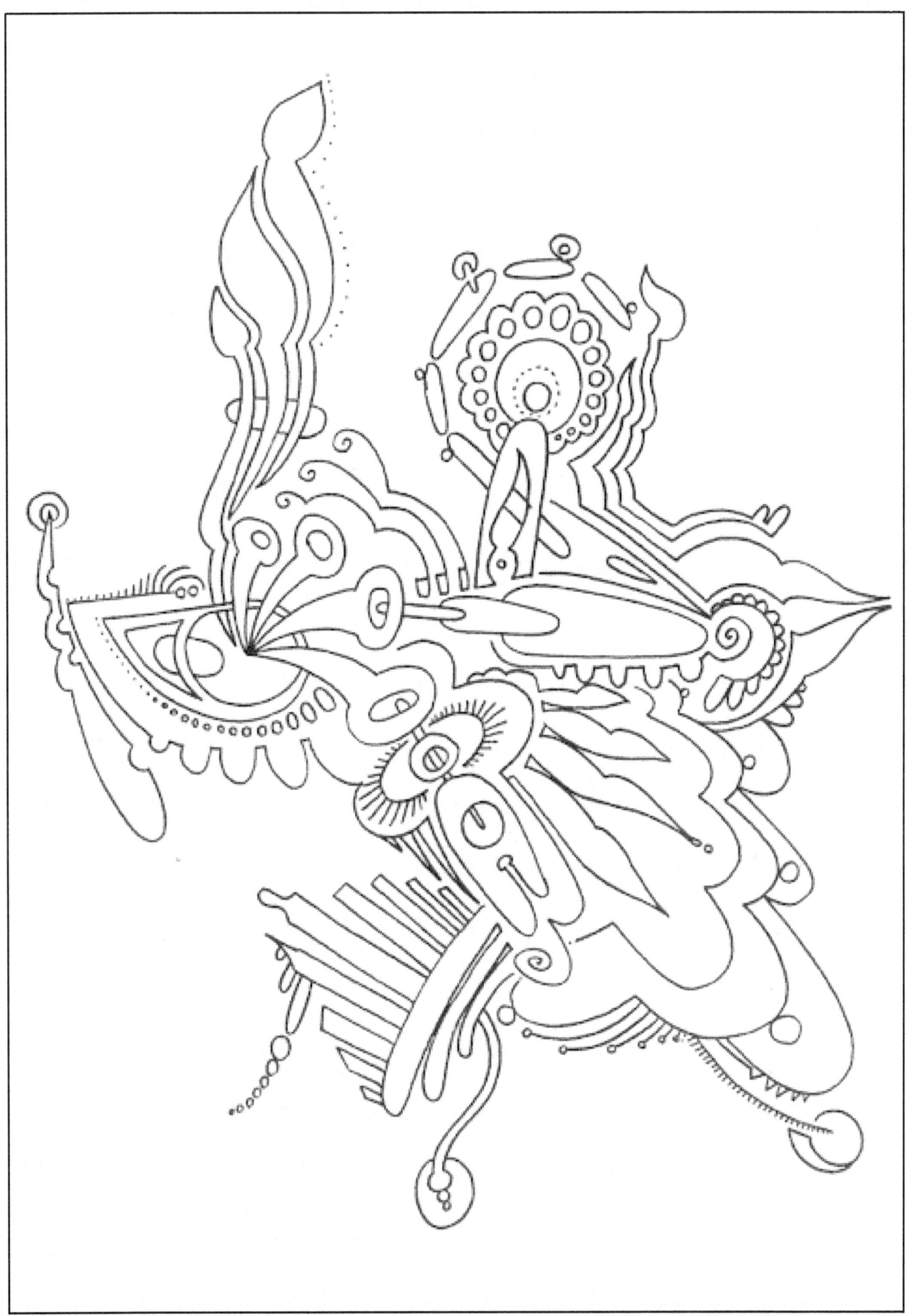

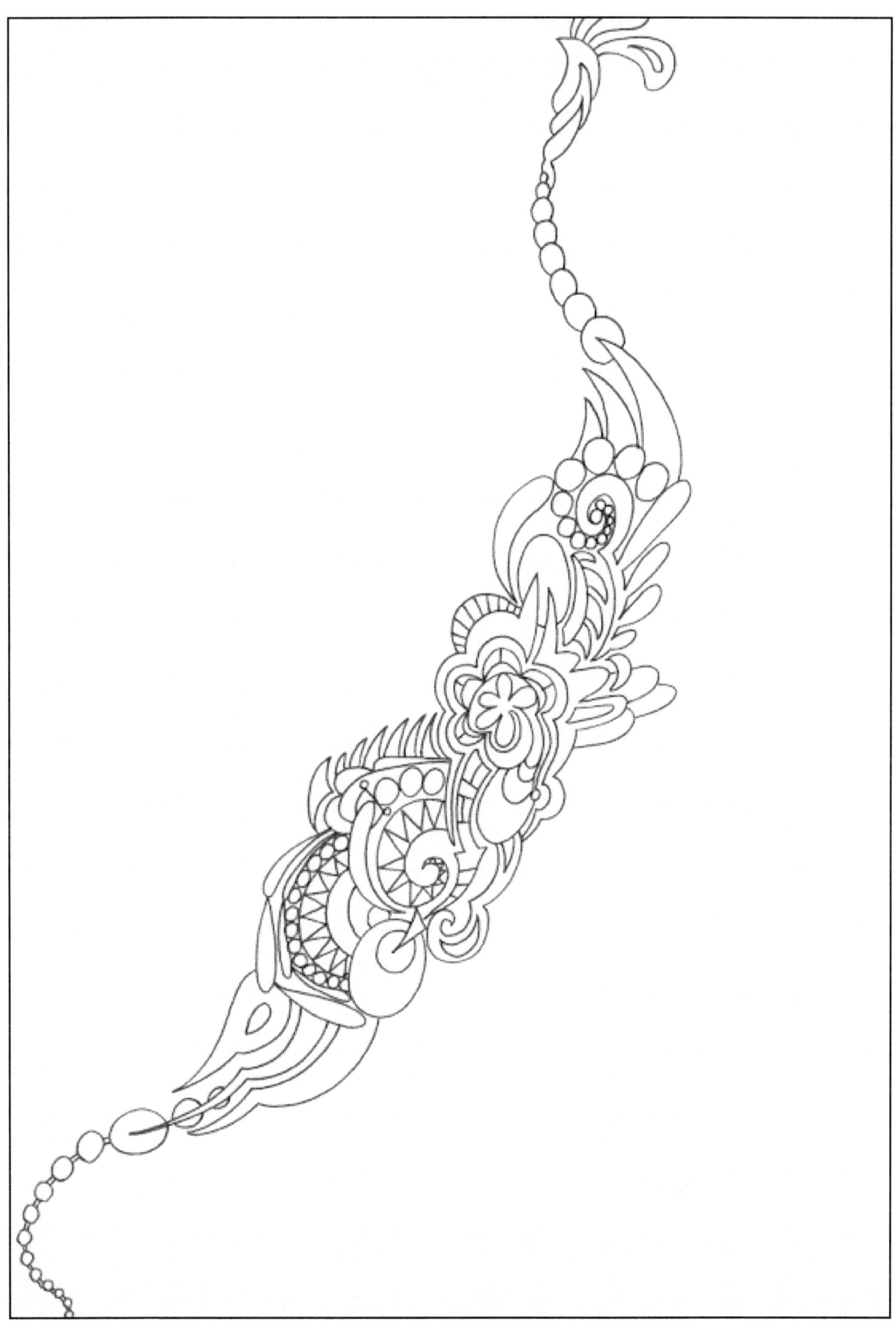

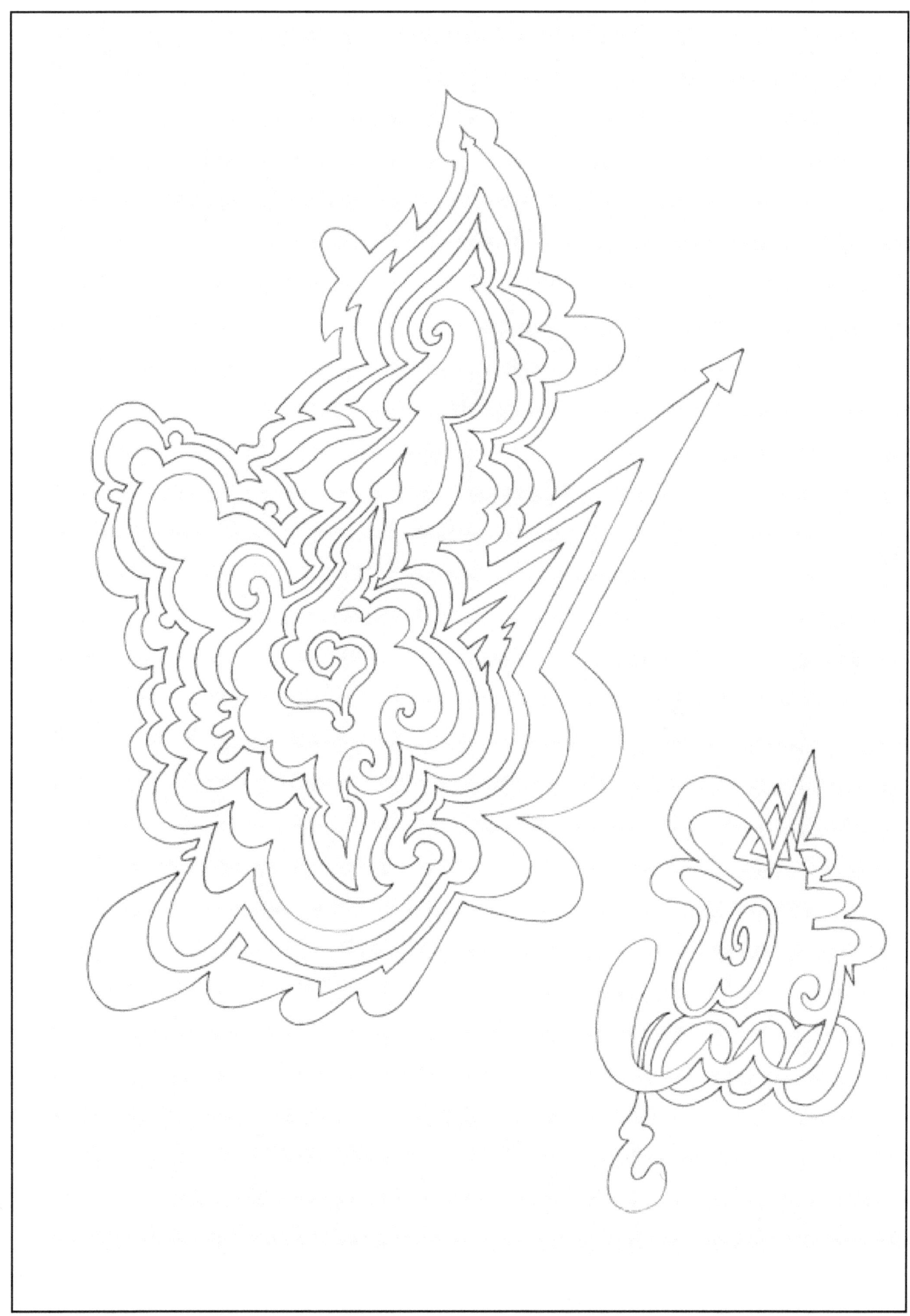

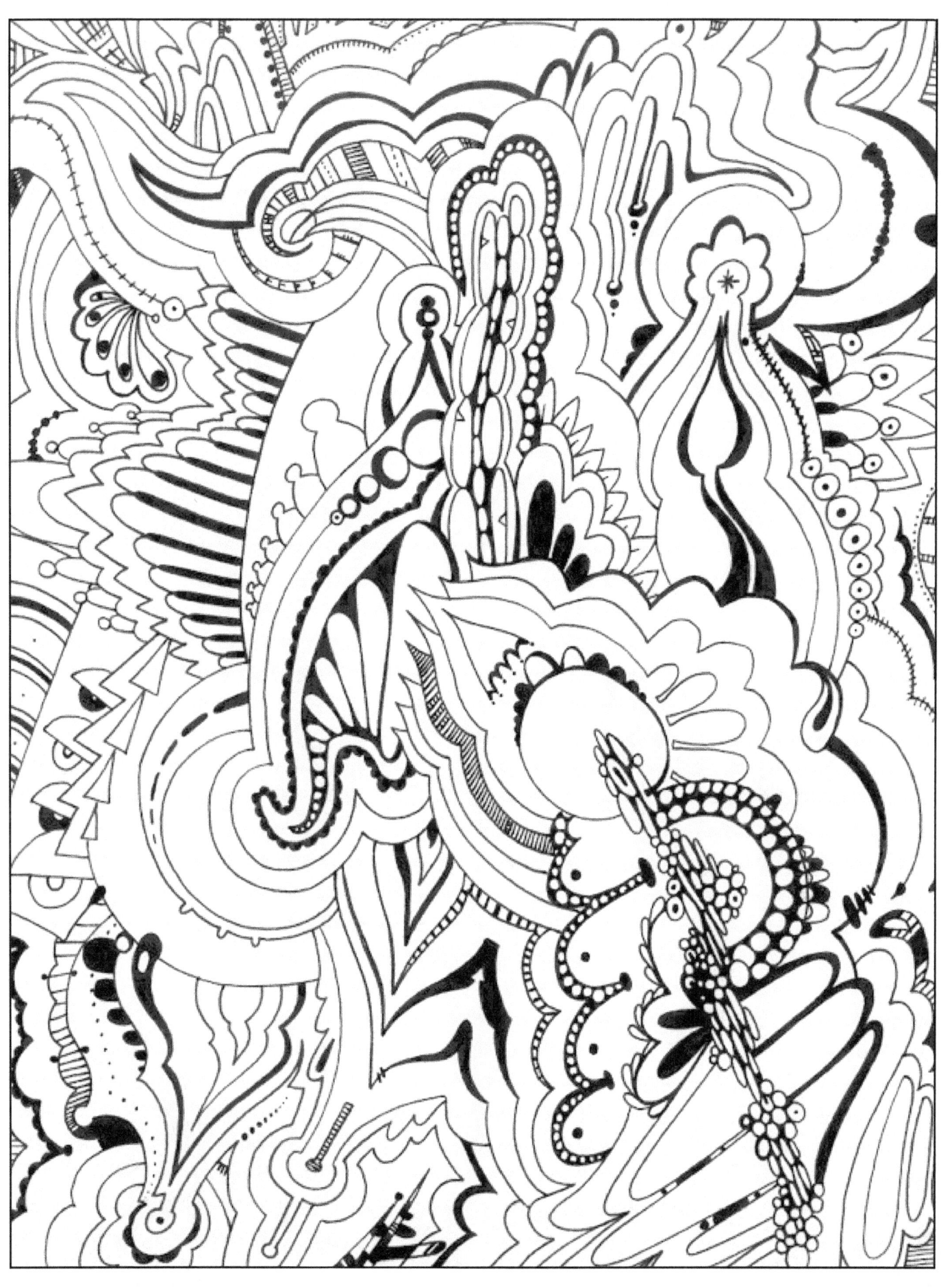

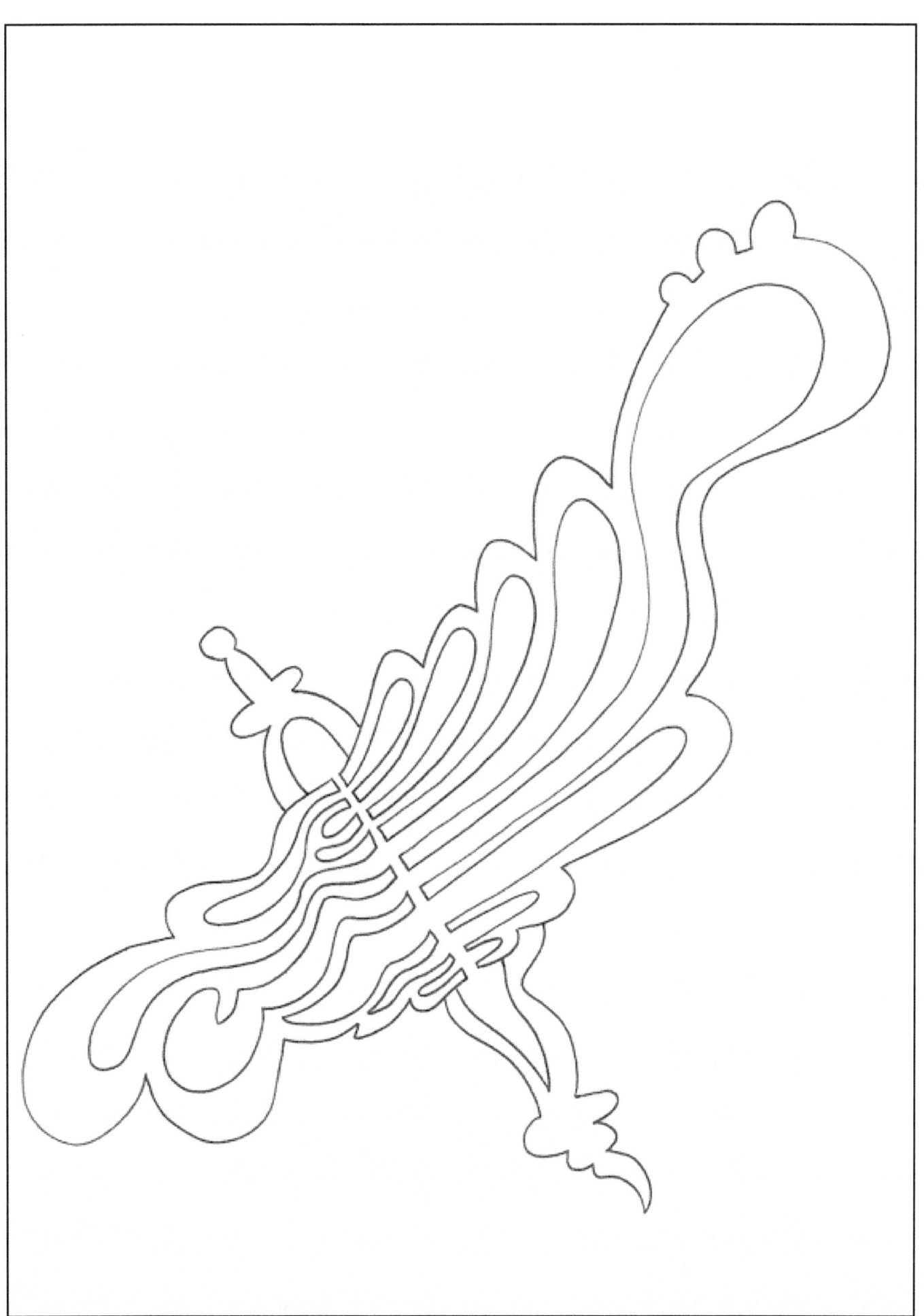

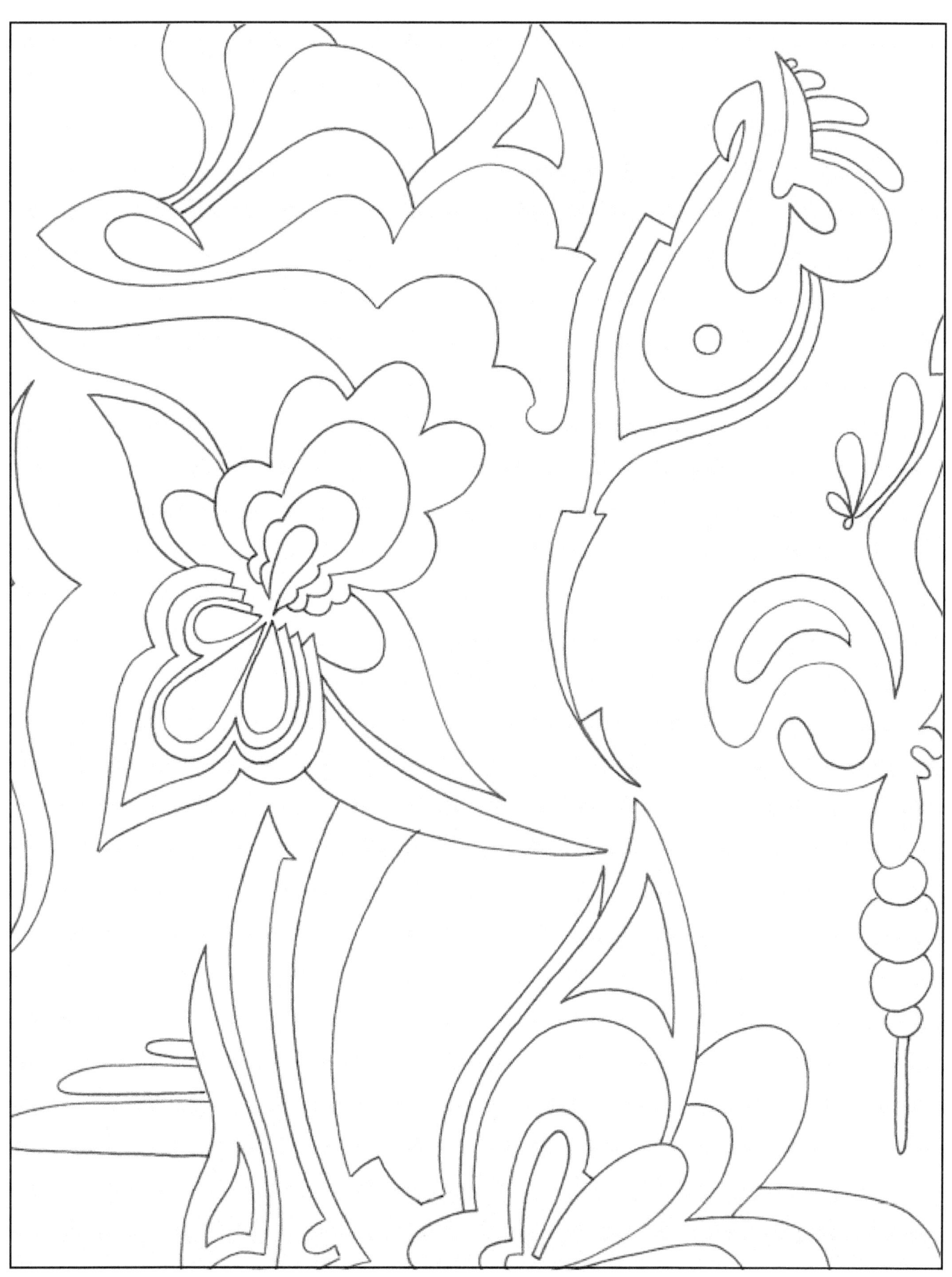

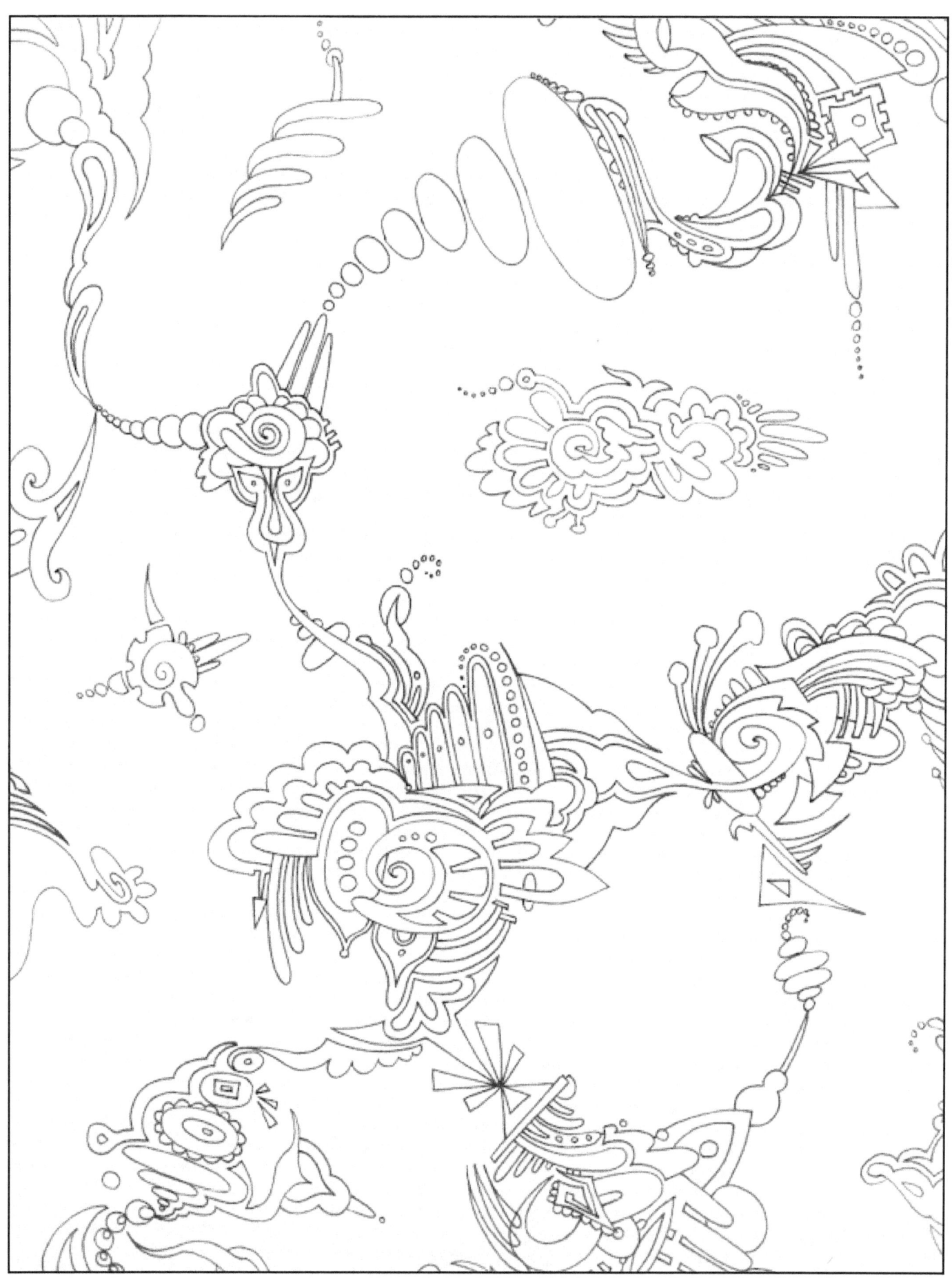

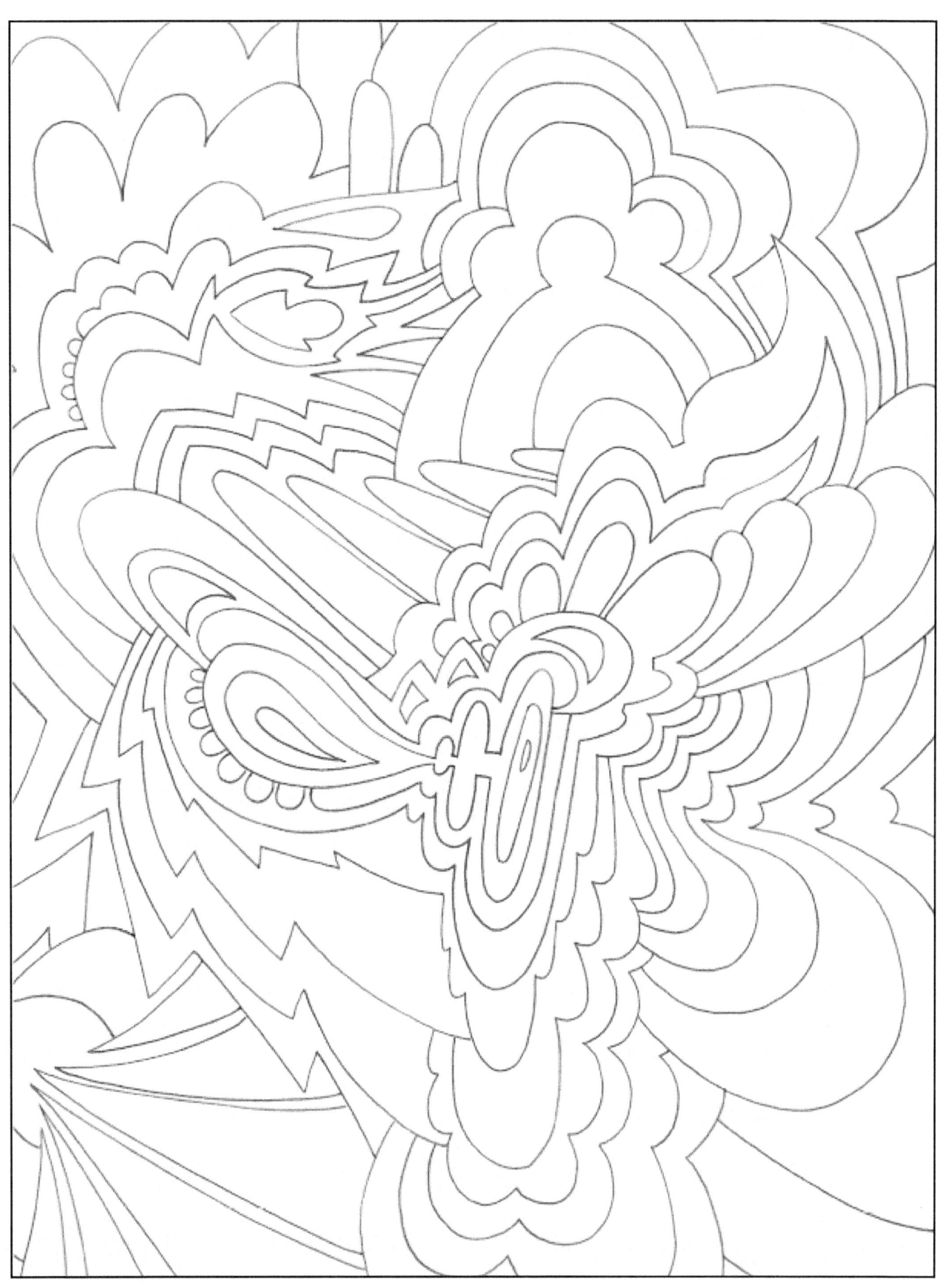

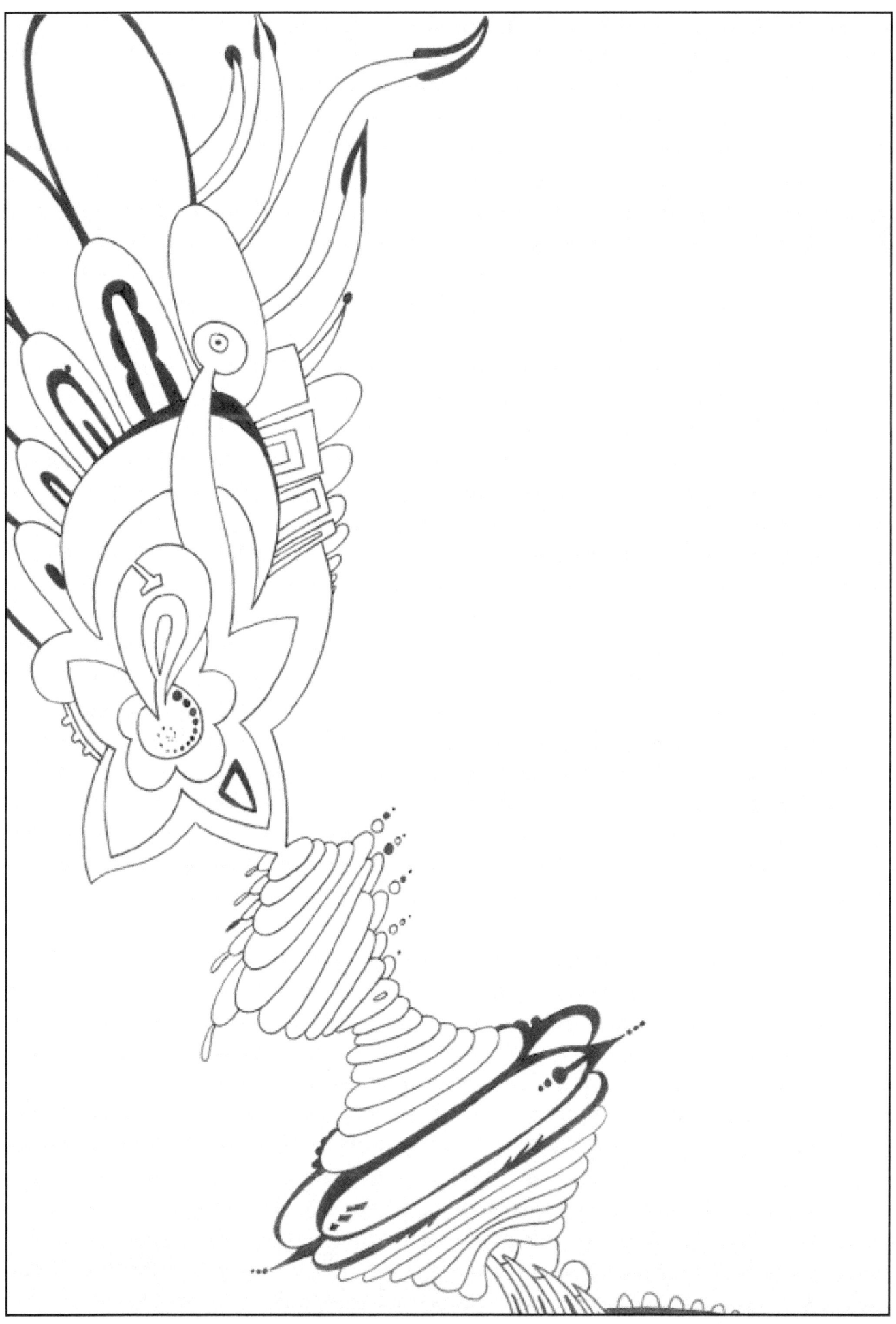

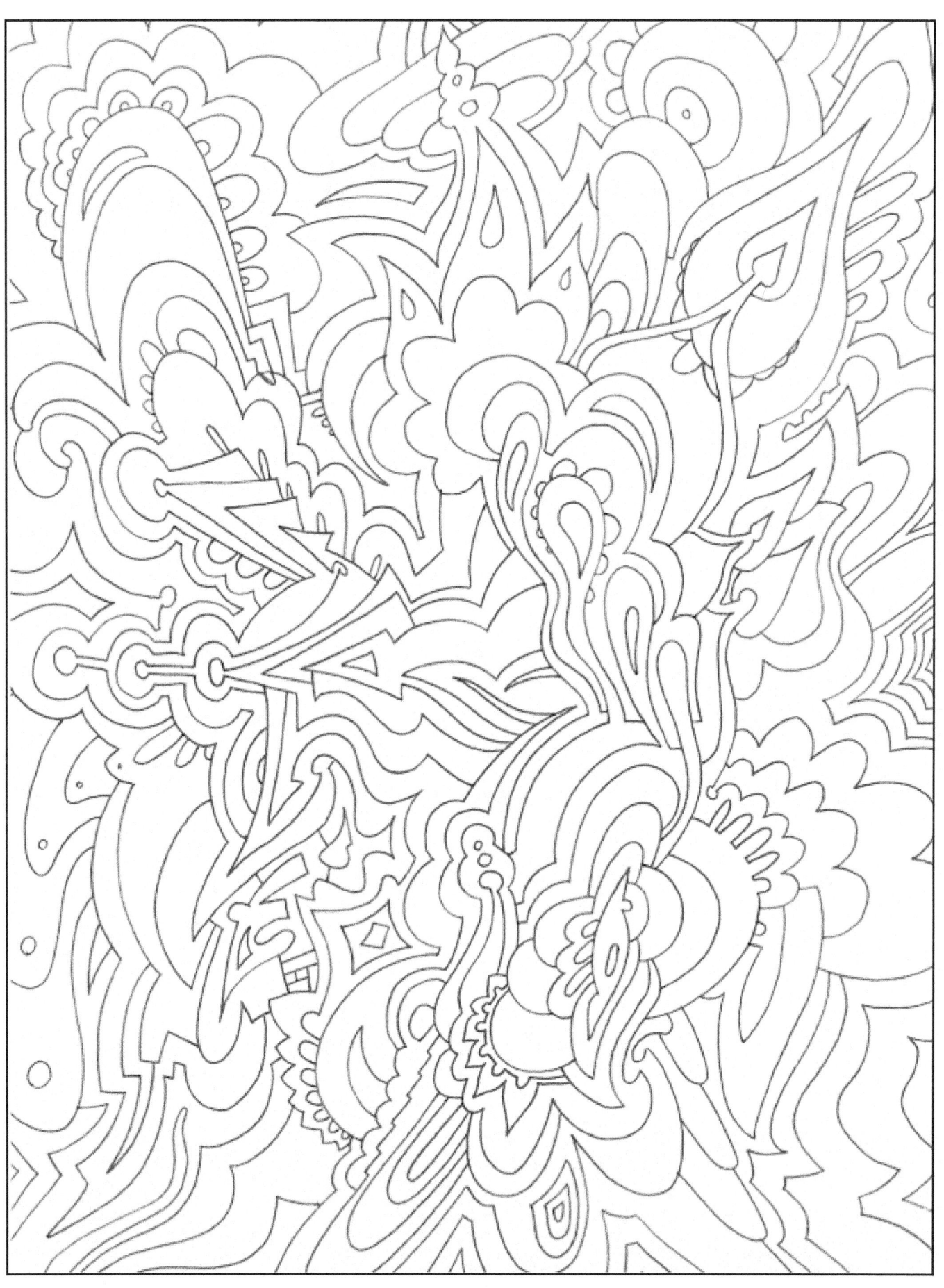

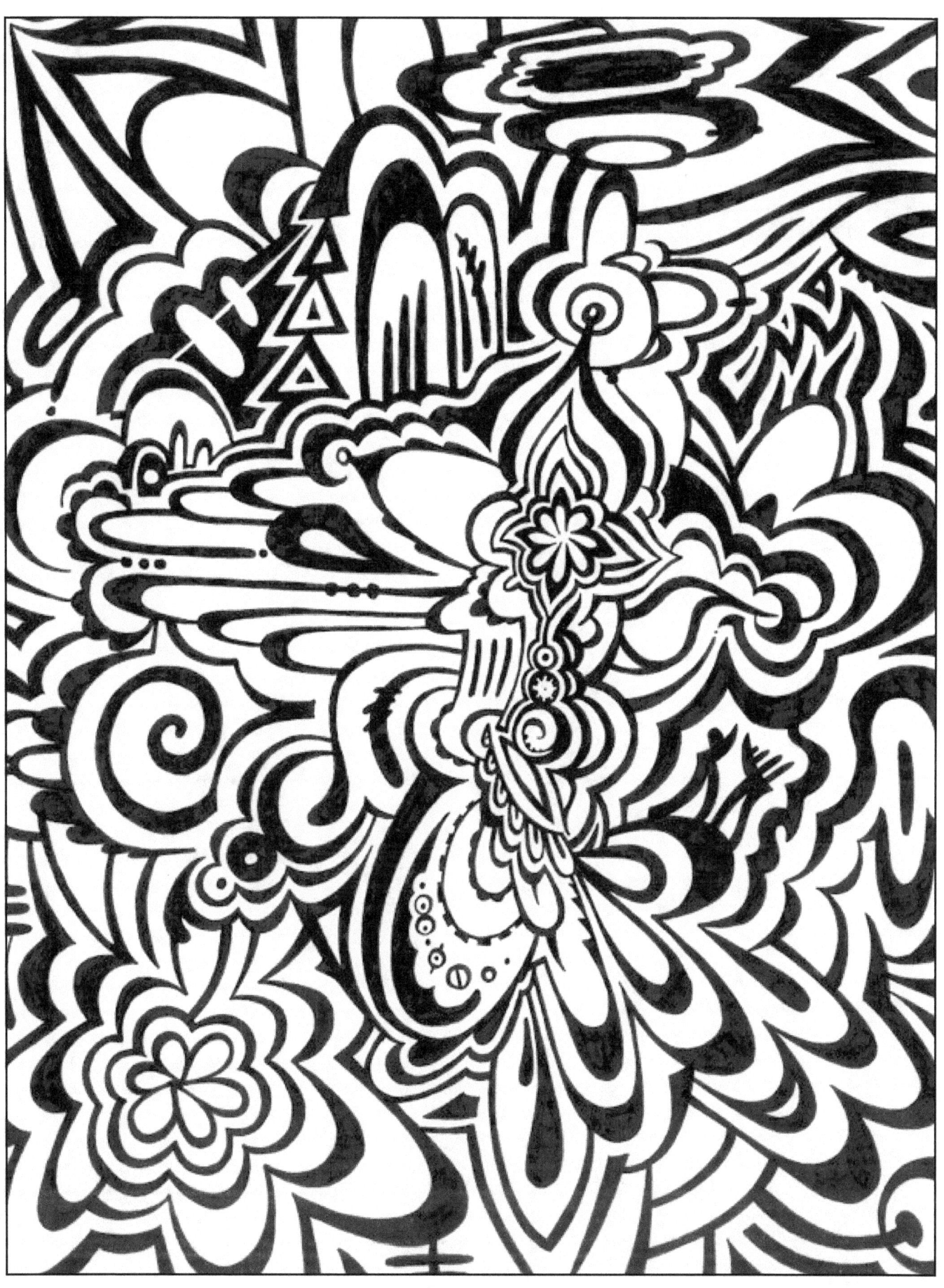

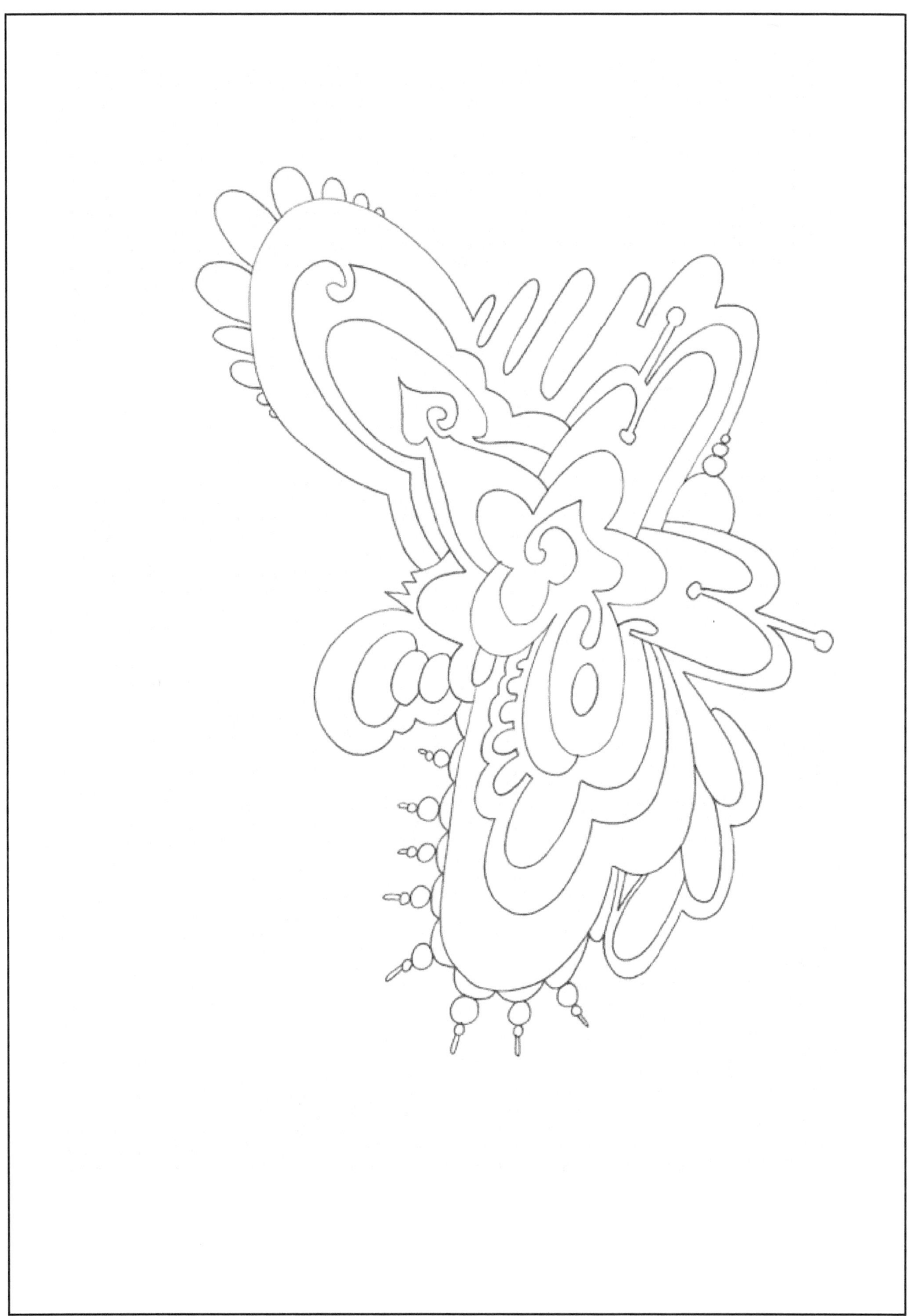

www.ingramcontent.com/pod-product-compliance
Lightning Source LLC
Chambersburg PA
CBHW081503170526
45166CB00008B/2531